BLACK LOVE, BLACK HATE

BLACK LOVE, BLACK HATE

INTIMATE ANTAGONISMS IN
AFRICAN AMERICAN LITERATURE

FELICE D. BLAKE

THE OHIO STATE UNIVERSITY PRESS

COLUMBUS

Copyright © 2018 by The Ohio State University.
All rights reserved.

Library of Congress Cataloging-in-Publication Data available online at https://catalog.loc.gov/

Cover design by Larry Nozik
Text design by Juliet Williams
Type set in Adobe Minion Pro

CONTENTS

Acknowledgments vii

INTRODUCTION 1

CHAPTER 1 The Public Space of Intimate Antagonisms: Black Intimacy and Opposition to Jim Crow 27

CHAPTER 2 Intimate Antagonisms and Double Consciousness in the Debate over Integration 55

CHAPTER 3 Going to Bed Angry: Intimate Antagonisms in the Epoch of Black Power 85

CHAPTER 4 What's Yours Is Mine: The Paradox of Intraracial "Bootstrap" Politics 117

EPILOGUE Intimate Antagonisms, the Undercommons, and the Town-Hall Meeting 141

Bibliography 151
Index 161

ACKNOWLEDGMENTS

I AM both ecstatic and humbled by the opportunity to thank the many people who have supported the development and completion of this project. The notion that someone has ideas worth putting into a book always presumes that there is some group to whom one is writing, which makes the work lively and conversational. This is always an attempt to communicate across time, space, and differences, intimate or otherwise. Thankfully (pun intended), acknowledgment pages are opportunities to express gratitude to those who made the process worthwhile and to do so with abandon!

Toni Morrison has been one of the most important figures in my development as a writer and intellectual. Although we have never met and I don't know how often authors thank her in their acknowledgments, I am so honored to be able to do so in mine for her extraordinary impact on my life. Thank you for your relationship with words, your creation of space, and your love of Black people.

Tremendous gratitude goes to The Ohio State University Press, its editorial board, Editor-in-Chief Kristen Elias Rowley, and the spirited reviewers of this manuscript. Your collective support of this project has made this a wonderful creative and productive process. Appreciation is also due to the institutional support I received during the process of researching and writing this manuscript. I am honored to have been a University of California President's Postdoctoral Fellow mentored by Dr. Abdul Jan Mohamed at UC Berkeley. I am also thankful for the Regents Junior and Regents Humanities Faculty Fellowships I received from the College of Letters and Science at the University of California, Santa Barbara. In addition to this support, I am also grateful for the Interdisciplinary Humanities Center Release Time and the Faculty Career Development Awards I received from UCSB. Such support extended to UCSB's English department and its extraordinary championing of me as well as my scholarly and activist work. Special recognition is due to Drs. Bishnupriya Ghosh, Stephanie Batiste, Julie Carlson, Aranye Fradenburg Joy, Glyn Salton-Cox, and Enda Duffy. I am also buoyed by the spirit of generosity and support I've experienced across UCSB. Special thanks goes to the Departments of Feminist Studies, Black Studies, and Global Studies, the Center for Black Studies Research, the Hemispheric Souths Research Center, the American Cultures and Global Contexts Center, and the MultiCultural Center and its exceptional director Zaveeni Khan-Marcus. I am also so thankful for the professional, personal, and creative sustenance from my many colleagues, including Nadège Clitandre, Claudine Michel, Mireille Miller-Young, Lisa Hajjar, Laila Sheeren, Sherene Seikaly, Paul Amar, Eileen Boris, and Diane Fujino. Our colleague and ancestor Clyde Woods always reminded me to write something that the community needs and can use. I hope that this project contributes to that important work.

I am forever thankful to the students who enthusiastically volunteered to participate in UCSB's Faculty Research Program (FRAP) with me and in connection to this project. I am grateful for the learning and memories developed with Julia Olson, Cristina Roman, and Simrun Bhagat. I am also grateful to the students of Feminist Studies 185 (2008) and English 197 (2011) for their courageous exploration of Black sexual politics and depictions of intraracial intimacy.

Victor Rios and Rebeca Mireles are friends and colleagues who have helped me to hold it down in the most important way. There's no number of pages that could contain my gratitude to you, Maya,

Nina, and Marco. This project is possible because of your presence in my and my daughter's lives.

My manuscript workshop was one of the best writing experiences I've ever had. Thank you for the participation, comments, and generosity from Arlene Keizer, George Lipsitz, Paula Ioanide, Julie Carlson, Geoffrey Jacques, Chandan Reddy, Barbara Tomlinson, Alison Reed, Swati Rana, and Fred Moten. None of you can begin to imagine the BBQ my parents have planned! I'm also grateful to the many other people who have taken time to comment and/or reflect on the project with me, including Karen Lund, Barbara Walker, and Alex Lubin.

Special thanks is due to George Lipsitz, who has helped me to shape the direction of this project through conversations and interactions over many years. Thank you for accompanying me and for your model of mentorship.

I'm eternally grateful to be "just friends" with Julie Carlson and for her extraordinary commitment to my work and well-being. Aranye Fradenburg Joy and Eileen Fradenburg Joy created an incredible space for me to lean back, laugh, and learn. I'm so appreciative of this most special form of care. Kay Young has been a champion of me and this project from the first day we met. I'm so grateful for all of the meaningful ways our paths have always crossed.

Rhynna Santos and Kenia Calderon have stuck with me for the long haul and celebrated every accomplishment along the way. I'm so thankful for your friendship and looking forward to the next fête! To Paula Ioanide, thank you for coming into my life for this leg of life's journey. I'm blessed to know you, humbled by what we learn together, and excited for the next chapters. Alison Reed and Mary McGuire are awesome friends who always appreciate how the music helps everything else make sense.

I have an incredible family who have *all* contributed love, babysitting, encouragement, meals, and enthusiasm towards the completion of this project. Thank you to my sisters Deborah Blake, Carol Barnes, Kelly Blake Wiseman, and Sandra Blake-Lange. My nieces Brittani White, Ashley Barnes, Sidne Lange, and Alyssa Barnes and nephews Justin White and Joshua Lange have also been wonderful interlocutors and advocates during sleepovers at my house and family gatherings in the United States and abroad. This familial spirit of encouragement and support has been fostered and modeled by my wonderful parents, Kell Blake and Dorothy Blake. I am forever grateful for their examples of spirited debate, intellectual curiosity, and Black love.

To Malena Blake Kleiven, our time and existence together are the motivation, celebration, catalyst, and spark for all that matters to me. This book is dedicated to you.

INTRODUCTION

> *Sullen, irritable, he cultivated his hatred of Darlene. Never did he once consider directing his hatred toward the hunters. Such an emotion would have destroyed him. They were big, white, armed men. He was small, black, helpless. His subconscious knew what his conscious mind did not guess—that hating them would have consumed him.... He was, in time, to discover that hatred of white men—but not now. Not in impotence, but later, when the hatred could find sweet expression. For now, he hated the one who had created the situation, the one who bore witness to his failure, his impotence. The one whom he had not been able to protect, to spare.*
>
> —Toni Morrison, *The Bluest Eye*, 150–51

THE EPIGRAPH from Toni Morrison's *The Bluest Eye*[1] reveals just how complicated the notion of bonding over shared suffering can be. At this point in the novel Cholly and Darlene have just been discovered making love by White hunters who shine their flashlights on the couple and insist that they finish the act for the amusement of their tormentors. The couple's shared experience of racist, sexual violence results in degrees of shame, humiliation, and helplessness that produce a rupture between the would-be lovers. Cholly's feeling of racialized powerlessness finds expression in aggression and hatred directed toward Darlene, and eventually to other Black females rather than toward the White men. He does not experience her, in this scene, as being subject to the racism that they both endure. He does not see how he has become an instrument of her rape or how she is forced to bear his shame. He does not see how their relations with each other have been shaped by the structures of racist and misogynist violence.

---

1. Cited parenthetically throughout.

The Bluest Eye portrays how the fierce imposition of White supremacy positions Black people as witnesses to and symbols of each other's degradation. Metaphorically, the hunters violate Cholly with their lamps and guns, and weaponize his body in Darlene's brutalization. Cholly's attempt to "kneel" and Darlene's attempt to shroud her face reveal their coerced prostration in the face of racist violence, and the ways that the would-be lovers turn away from each other (148). Morrison's novel reveals how, from the perspective of the White gaze, Black intimacy should function exclusively as an extension of White supremacy. In response, Cholly hates "the one who had created the situation, the one who bore witness to his failure, his impotence. The one whom he had not been able to protect" (151). Hatred and shame between Darlene and Cholly reveal how the negotiation of racial violence can manifest in intimate, intraracial antagonisms.

Intimate antagonisms in the novel function nevertheless as a generative trope that repurposes racially produced tensions *intraracially* and in potentially radical ways. What is most salient in Morrison's work is that she never presents the White gaze as totalizing in the exposure and depiction of Black vulnerability. For example, the scene of the hunters' sadism is intercut by that of the funeral for Cholly's Aunt Jimmy, a member of a generation of Black women who highlight the paradoxes of apparent vulnerability. The narrative positions these Black women as central to the community and their relationship to Cholly and Darlene as equally important (if not more so) to the reading of the young couple's encounter with the hunters. In other words, the relationship between Black people challenges the White gaze and its exploitative perspective on Black intimacy. The narrator describes these women's complex lives:

> White women said, "Do this." White children said, "Give me that." White men said, "Come here." Black men said, "Lay down." The only people they need not take orders from were black children and each other. But they took all of that and re-created it in their own image. They ran the houses of white people, and knew it. When white men beat their men, they cleaned up the blood and went home to receive

abuse from the victim. They beat their children with one hand and stole for them with the other. (139)

Aunt Jimmy belongs to a generation of working-class Black people situated as pillars of the community—a community defined by Black women's stoic patience, duty, and long-suffering. The narrator underlines their structural disadvantage through their confinement to servile labor in a racist and sexist labor market, as well as their subjection to racial and gender violence from people outside of and from within their community. Nonetheless, these women are also the visionaries and creators of community, taking all that they witness and endure and recreating "it in their own image." The collective consciousness and shared sense of obligation that the women develop is what enables them to clean up the blood spilled from the brutalities of racial terror and, paradoxically, to "beat their children with one hand" and steal "for them with the other." By deliberately rejecting dominant discourses of Black familial and sexual pathology, *The Bluest Eye* concerns itself with intraracial, intimate relations that foreground the power and possibilities that Black radicalism signifies for Black people.

It is from Aunt Jimmy's funeral—and the community members' presence there—that Cholly feels love ("Cholly was still the major figure, because he was 'Jimmy's Boy, the last thing she loved'") and thus confident to steal himself away in Darlene's company (140). Footfalls away from the communal celebration of Aunt Jimmy's life, Cholly and Darlene, representatives of the new rebellious generation in the community, are thwarted in their sexual maturation by the dictates of White heteropatriarchy. The epigraph that begins this introduction appears *after* Cholly returns to Aunt Jimmy's house, recalling the trauma having been instrumentalized by the White hunters: "Afraid of running into Darlene, he would not go far from the house, but neither could he endure the atmosphere of his dead Aunt's house" (150). Cholly's experience of racial and sexual terror compels him to run away from the *Black* gaze and from the spaces where the reflection of his pain, humiliations, and potential would be made palpable. Running away from and rejecting the possibilities for intraracial vulnerability result in intimate antagonisms that remove Cholly from community and render him a menace to its formation and health.

This alienation creates the fomenting conditions for his brutal exploitation of his daughter Pecola. The scene of what Cholly interprets as his "rape" by the hunters (even though he *and* Darlene have been violated) is structurally connected to his subsequent rape of his daughter—the instance of violence at the center of Morrison's novel. The sense of shame and humiliation Cholly learns to feel about desire provokes a confused and uncomfortable emotion in him that mixes hatred with tenderness (163). He interprets Black women's (and his own daughter's) misery under the regimes of racialized poverty and gendered bigotry as a clear accusation against him (161). The possibilities of love, mutual care, and affection are undermined by deep insecurities within him. The effects of racial tragedy and trauma are shown to divide more often than unite the Black family members, friends, and lovers who populate Morrison's novel. Such scenes of intimate antagonisms pervade Black literature.

INTIMATE ANTAGONISMS AND A BLACK RADICAL TRADITION OF READING

Black Love, Blake Hate describes how literary representations of intraracial, intimate antagonisms participate in the development of collective consciousness within the Black radical tradition and nurture both communal bonds *and* communal critique. The fiction examined in this book, written from the 1920s to the present, participates in what Cedric Robinson has called the Black radical tradition, a process of dialogue, debate, and struggle that also recognizes the political meaning of Black experience. The Black radical tradition entails the creation and cultivation of ways of being (ontology) and ways of knowing (epistemology) central to the evolution of Black humanity *even as* Black people grapple with the impositions and restrictions of racial capitalism. Writing by Black authors composes part of what

Robinson describes as the intergenerational "accretion" and transference of knowledge from struggle.² As seen with Aunt Jimmy and her generation of women in *The Bluest Eye*, it is part of the tradition that Robinson defines as "a collective consciousness informed by the historical struggles for liberation and motivated by the shared sense of obligation to preserve the collective being."³ This conception of the Black radical tradition incorporates everyday instances of resistance to subordination as well as their connection to broader understandings of oppression.

Black Love, Black Hate builds on Robinson's definition by considering how Black literature portrays the process of creating collectivity as sometimes tense or even chaotic, but always necessary. It insists on the richness of that complex negotiation. Even in eras of overt racist exclusion—like the New Negro Renaissance period of the early twentieth century—Black writers have ruminated on what holistic visions of community might look like. The authors whose work forms the core objects of study in this book operate under and insist upon the fracturing of blackness and facile notions of community that generate complex processes for negotiating alternative terms of Black humanity and collectivity.

Robinson identifies root causes of the intraracial refusals and rejections in a historical schism in the Black community between an assimilationist wing steeped in capitalist ambition and individualism, and an alternative political culture emerging from slavery and peonage that Robinson describes as "inventive rather than imitative, communitarian rather than individualistic, democratic rather than republican and Afro-Christian rather than secular and materialist."⁴ By contextualizing issues of normativity and nonnormativity through the inventive and imaginative frame of the Black radical tradition, we see how intimate antagonisms generate contrary texts in terms of both representation and form. A novel like *The Bluest Eye*

---

2. Cedric Robinson, *Black Marxism: The Making of the Black Radical Tradition* (Chapel Hill: University of North Carolina Press, 2005).
3. Ibid., 171.
4. Cedric Robinson, *Black Movements in America* (New York: Routledge, 1997), 97.

presents readers with images that we can't or don't want to see. In what context can the antagonisms that produce incest and misogyny be analyzed without seeming to sanction the dominant discourse of Black-on-Black violence and pathology? Incest patrols the boundaries at the limits of culture and becomes, symbolically, the thing that cannot (must not) be enacted, seen, or spoken. As Hortense Spillers points out, "it is only in fiction—and perhaps the psychoanalytic session—that incest as dramatic enactment and sexual economy can take place at all."[5] Such contrariness in the realm of fictional representations disrupts the presumptions of what we think we know and what we think can be said about Black social life. Depictions of intimate, intraracial antagonisms fracture the boundaries that reinforce the hegemony of the traditional nuclear family (normativity) or its incestuous opposite (pathology). In my reading, these intimate antagonisms open new fields of experimentation and new forms of language for imagining the radical possibilities of Black life.

The Bluest Eye exposes the gendered and racial logic of White supremacy, but it also challenges the respectability politics of Black activism for its reluctance to contend with intraracial fractures and vulnerabilities. The development, maturation, growth, and extension of the Black radical tradition demand a holistic engagement with the contours and shifts of Black experience. Neither Cholly Breedlove's wish for recognition nor his subsequent behavior exhibits subservience to dominant demands for sexual and gender normativity; nonetheless, his attitude and actions figure prominently as object lessons about intimate antagonisms. Cholly's situation exposes an impasse that my reconsideration of twentieth-century Black literature helps us to confront: the politics of Black respectability, in its desire for normativity, prevent a full analysis, and thus a potential overturning, of the many scenes of intraracial intimate conflict to which Black literature and lives bear witness.

Underlying *Black Love, Black Hate* is the claim that Black creative writers' depictions of intraracial conflict demonstrate a certain inten-

---

5. Hortense Spillers, "'The Permanent Obliquity of an In(pha)llibly Straight': In the Time of the Daughters and the Fathers," in *Black, White, and in Color: Essays on American Literature and Culture* (1989; Chicago: University of Chicago Press, 2003), 231.

tional and strategic indifference to the White gaze. If these works were written exclusively for White readers, their authors might have been hesitant to promulgate negative representations of their community. But because expressive culture is a crucial public sphere for Black people, often the only or most vital sphere of public life, Black authors face a uniquely difficult situation. From Horace Pippin's efforts to construct an alternative textual lexicon of Black suffering and struggle in his paintings and prose to Toni Morrison's insistent construction of an alternative archive of re-memory in her novels, creative Black artists have used expressive culture as a means of convening a town meeting that cannot meet anywhere else.[6] They recognize cultural work as one of the few endeavors where it is possible to forge textual and ideological critiques of White supremacy and its extensive effects on Black people, but also as a site where Black people can take stock of the degree to which they have internalized elements of the poisonous pathologies used to oppress them. In a society that suppresses organic oral traditions, commodifies culture, co-opts grassroots creativity, and shrinks institutions open to Black voices and interests, this is a serious challenge. Black literature is a crucial forum for devising, airing, and evaluating these terms. And its efficacy as a witness to the complexity of Black lives depends on the depth of its probing of the language being redesigned by Black artists to convey it.

Portrayals of intraracial conflict in Black literature challenge the long-standing assumption that political unity and singularity are preconditions for Black radical politics. A unified notion of racial community informed efforts by Black people to wage their collective struggles for social justice, racial equality, and civic inclusion. Ending de jure segregation, securing voting rights, and shaping a shared identity as an aggrieved and insurgent people rested on appreciation of a linked fate that required reciprocal recognition. To be sure, collective mobilizations around linked fates and common interests have led to important victories for race justice framed through strug-

---

6. See Celeste-Marie Benier, *Suffering and Sunset: World War I in the Art and Life of Horace Pippin* (Philadelphia: Temple University Press, 2015), and Danille Kathleen Taylor-Guthrie, ed., *Conversations with Toni Morrison* (Jackson: University Press of Mississippi, 1994).

gles for what Cathy Cohen describes as consensus issues.[7] All Black people benefited from the success of struggles for consensus issues such as the end of slavery, laws against lynching, ending racially specific impediments to education, serving on juries, and voting. But consensus issues coexist with what Cohen calls cross-cutting issues, issues such as ending domestic violence, authorizing marriage and adoption equality for gays and lesbians, or ensuring reproductive justice. It is in the realm of cross-cutting issues that intimate antagonisms take place and encouraging a deep meditation on them where the Black radical tradition will advance its commitment to freedom.

Literary depictions of intimate antagonisms reveal how intraracial aggression and abandonment reproduce the ill effects of racial injustice. The epistemological frame privileged by the Black radical tradition argues that the whole group is damaged when it is ruled by the interests of a few. Uniting around glorified ideals of the prosperous and properly gendered nuclear family squanders the insights and energies emanating from the experiences of the many different kinds of intimate relations constructed through affinity groups, extended and invented families, and homosocial settings. Because they reveal problems inside the community that have been largely unidentified and therefore unsolved, such as the problems produced by racism's intersectional amplifications of classism, sexism, and homophobia, the airing of intimate antagonisms provides a creative space for exposing, interrogating, and opposing the full reach and power of racism.

Representations of radical divisions inside the community appear again and again in Black American literature, in stories of incest (*The Bluest Eye,* 1970), domestic violence (*Native Son,* 1940), betrayal (*The Man Who Cried I Am,* 1967), dangerous secrets (*Silver Sparrow,* 2011), longing (*Go Tell It on the Mountain,* 1953), rejection (*Zami,* 1982), abandonment (*Their Eyes Were Watching God,* 1937), exploitation (*The Street,* 1946), addiction ("Sonny's Blues," 1957), and familial fragmentation (*Rebel Yell,* 2009). The radical unity celebrated in African American politics contrasts markedly with the radical divi-

---

7. Cathy Cohen, *The Boundaries of Blackness: AIDS and the Breakdown of Black Politics* (Chicago: University of Chicago Press, 1999).

siveness displayed in the literature. The intraracial recognition that lies at the heart of Black politics co-exists uneasily and uncomfortably with intraracial rejection and reciprocal recrimination in Black literature.

Of course, authors of all races, nationalities, and social identities are concerned with building reader investment and engagement and constructing narrative tension through accounts of conflict and ideological tension. The radical divisiveness of everyday life, however, takes on a specific meaning in texts about Black Americans. Centuries of slavery, segregation, and their successor systems of racial subordination have compelled Black people constantly to confront a linked fate, to face conditions they experience in common that leave them with a common destiny. Yet while artificially lumped together by the negative ascriptions and oppressive actions of White supremacy, Black people remain deeply divided. They differ by gender and generation, class and color, religion and region, sexuality and psychology. Fighting tactically and strategically against outside oppression has often required focusing on similarities and disregarding differences. Yet embracing what Chela Sandoval calls the "consensual illusion" of racial unity can permit and perpetuate internal oppressions against the parts of the group that are deemed weaker, less powerful, and nonnormative.[8] Kevin Gaines and other historians of the Black experience have delineated how Black elites in the late nineteenth and early twentieth centuries promoted "a culture of uplift" that portrayed the progress of all Black people as identical to their own aspirations and interests, that made the health of the Black community synonymous with the well-being of its wealthier, more educated, lighter skinned, and gender-normative part of the community.[9] Thus Black progress was yoked to a hierarchy that elevated rich over poor, urban over rural, light over dark, male over female, and straight over gay.

Black women writers have been especially perceptive about the ways that calls for race loyalty have been mechanisms for suppress-

---

8. Chela Sandoval, *Methodology of the Oppressed* (Minneapolis: University of Minnesota Press, 2000), 63.

9. Kevin Gaines, *Uplifting the Race: Black Leadership, Politics, and Culture in the Twentieth Century* (Chapel Hill: University of North Carolina Press, 1996).

ing demands for gender justice. Black queer writers have recognized how seeking group respect through performances of bourgeois respectability has entailed elite disavowal of nonconforming and nonnormative gender and sexual identities. A large part of the success of the Black freedom movement of the mid-twentieth century came from bridging these divisions. The organizing strategies of Ella Baker connected the culture of uplift to the culture of the blues, enabling both the pharmacist and the farm worker to join together in struggle. Fannie Lou Hamer promoted a political process that spoke to both the "sack toters" in the fields and the "grip (briefcase) toters" in law offices. In the final social justice battle of his life, Martin Luther King Jr. called for the "Negro haves" to join with the "Negro have-nots" in support of striking sanitation workers in Memphis, telling one audience that they needed a movement in which the man who has no house is considered as important as the man who went to Morehouse. Yet the fracturing of that coalition in the 1970s revealed the deep divisions that remained, promoting an efflorescence of fiction writing by Toni Morrison, Alice Walker, Gayl Jones, and other Black feminists seeking to call attention to the significance of intimate antagonisms.[10]

This book illustrates how this seeming contradiction is no contradiction at all, but instead evidence of a dialectical and dialogic relationship between intimate, intraracial antagonism and radical visions of liberation. *Black Love, Black Hate* addresses intraracial recognition and rejection as two sides of the same coin. The radical unity demanded by Black politics exacerbates the painful injuries inflicted by intraracial rejection in the microsocial sphere. The intraracial conflicts that occupy a central place in Black American fiction from the Great Black Migration to the contemporary post–civil rights era have augmented rather than undermined Black radical-

---

10. See Barbara Ransby, *Ella Baker and the Black Freedom Movement: A Radical Democratic Vision* (Chapel Hill: University of North Carolina Press, 2003); Martin Luther King Jr., *All Labor Has Dignity*, edited by Michael Honey (Boston: Beacon, 2011); Clarence Lang, *Black America in the Shadow of the Sixties: Notes on the Civil Rights Movement, Neoliberalism and Politics* (Ann Arbor: University of Michigan Press, 2015); Madhu Dubey, *Black Women Novelists and the Nationalist Aesthetic* (Bloomington: Indiana University Press, 1994); and Courtney Thorsson, *Women's Work: Nationalism and Contemporary African American Women's Novels* (Charlottesville: University Press of Virginia, 2013).

ism by underscoring the need to challenge internalized allegiances to hierarchy and exploitation in the course of struggles against external sources of oppression.

READING BLACK INTIMACIES

The act of reading scenes of intimate, intraracial conflicts produces both a memory of and a witness to the deepest secrets passed between bosom buddies and co-conspirators. As a metaphoric public forum, Black literature brings forth evidence and produces a witness, as we see in *The Bluest Eye*. A conversation takes place about Black humanity that is not simply about internalized racism but also about what language and vocabulary can best represent and affirm Black lives.

The complexity of *intraraciality* is thus a significant trope in Black literature. Reading this trope forces a reckoning between cultural and political struggles by meditating on the tensions between ethical and political representations of Black life configured in the public forum that Black literature creates. These stories enumerate the trope in particular ways at different moments of political urgency and insurgency. They feature subjects that are otherwise politically impossible, especially those who fail to conform to normative expectations for being, recognition, and value. The trope defamiliarizes the inside/outside of many things, including notions of belonging, home, race, and resistance. In the process, meaning-making refuses to conform to dominant ways of knowing that depend upon situating blackness in inferiority.

The contrariness of these intraracial depictions disrupts the racial mechanisms of literature as well. Morrison's *Playing in the Dark* interrogates how literary creation, artifice, and aesthetics revolve around a racial economy rooted in othering processes. Positing an "Africanist presence"—a fabricated and often phobic representation of blackness—that provides a basis on which to imagine and fashion the representation of the proper citizen subject,[11] these dynamics are

---

11. Toni Morrison, *Playing in the Dark: Whiteness and the Literary Imagination* (New York: Vintage Books, 1992), 6.

both the practiced and presumed function for national legitimation and inclusion. In other words, U.S. literature is always marked by its own creation of a racial other who is included in the realm of culture as the object and representation of abjection. Morrison asks how the supposed intellectual investment in the disciplinary boundaries of the field of literature then mimics and legitimates the material realities of racist exploitation existing inside and outside the ivory tower. While her argument focuses on the discipline of English specifically, she remains attentive to the reward structure in place that enables U.S. (and other) literary scholars to achieve and advance within the field without any recognition or examination of the role of racism, colonialism, or imperialism in the formation of Western literary traditions and cultural production. Assessing the work of Edith Wharton, Nathaniel Hawthorne, and Ernest Hemingway, Morrison's examples are taken not from marginal figures but from the very authors who compose the canon of U.S. literature. Pointing to the extraordinary work that these authors undertake to avoid endowing non-White personages with the literary and aesthetic markers of humanity, Morrison demands nothing less than our reassessment of the constitutive qualities of the racial tenets of the U.S. literary imagination.

Black literature has long performed this reassessment, but I contend that its portrayals of intimate antagonisms, in all their complexity and discomfort, are key to an adequate reassessment of Black literature's life-affirming possibilities. Each fracture and fissure creates within these fictional texts a more capacious notion of freedom than before. In this way, the trope of the intraracial exemplifies the very methodology of the Black radical tradition—of improvisation, conflict, and tension—that gives birth to renewed notions of creativity, freedom, and struggle. We need not see this fracturing as negative, therefore, but rather as a generative process that evolves Black consciousness and, by extension, all democratic visions. These antagonisms insist on keeping open the meaning and creation of community. The emphasis on intraracial relations is a way to signify that these are not representations of intraracial disharmony but mechanisms to disrupt the racial presumptions of literature as a field-critical study and cultural force.

Treatments of difference within a community marked by racial difference should not be aimed at reconciling the group so much as challenging the epistemological terms on which such degradations of gender, sexuality, class, and ability depend. They should foster a clash of epistemologies and lead to new conceptions of being and being together. I read the constant references to cross-cutting issues in Black literature as outlining the gaps, aporia, and lacunae that have resisted demands for a unity based in assimilation. Because of the long histories of sexual racism and racist sexism against African Americans, the realms of sexuality and private life are key zones for exerting control and envisioning freedom. Yet, in a society where racism and sexism remain hegemonic, even the freedom dreams of oppressed people can be structured in dominance. The airing of intimate antagonisms in literature demonstrates the ways that systemic hierarchy and exploitation "out there" can be internalized "in here." Even more important, authors indicate again and again that unless domestic contradictions *among* the people are addressed and adjudicated, there can be no meaningful public victory *for* the people. As hip-hop visionary Lauryn Hill phrases it, "how you gonna win if you ain't right within?" By emphasizing intimate antagonisms, authors temporarily and tactically deprioritize the color line as the primary axis for theorizing racial identity and experience.

The tendency in African American literature to repeat scenes of denigration, disavowal, and displeasure through accounts of intimate, intraracial conflict suggests that something essential is at play beyond the pleasure principle. In the context of the chaos of history, the legacy of shared suffering but also successes among Black people, representations of intimate antagonisms signal the return of the repressed, revisiting scenes of trauma and tragedy in the hope that they can be understood, managed, manipulated, and put to good use.

Intimate antagonisms, as I conceive them, are often overlooked because of the traditional focus on the color line, the discourses of Black-on-Black crime, and color-blind ideology. Discussions about racism frame Black people as victims needing solely to cross the color line by articulating their grievances in efforts to gain compensation for their suffering from racist offenses and misrecognition. The color line, which W. E. B. Du Bois used to describe the material and metaphoric representation of racial segregation and enmity, has long shaped critical approaches to the study of literature as well as the field of literature itself. The color line symbolizes racial inequality and the ideology of Black inferiority that justifies and masks racially determined disparities. In other words, racial separation requires denying Black humanity and misrecognizing Blacks as perverse or pathological. The "color line," its very existence and maintenance, depends upon the refusal to see a complex Black humanity and the resulting search for recognition.

Fiction has been a key site for interrogating the hegemony of whiteness specifically in the production, publication, and canonization of U.S. literature and more generally throughout society. Fiction has served as the ground for examining the possibilities for writers of color to speak a truer word about themselves in opposition to the pervasive and entrenched representations of their inferiority. Fiction has also been a privileged object for the presumed revelation of voice, agency, and resistance among those who have been silenced and constrained by the operations of gendered racial power. In content, form, and circulation, Black American creative work has been a valued asset in fashioning and articulating a poetics and aesthetics of struggle, resistance, and opposition.

Literature is a mediating mechanism, *not* a transparent window into individual or collective experiences and aspiration. Analyzing the social significance of literary texts is a complex task. Literary texts reflect their social and historical contexts, but they are not simple reductions of social relations. Literary texts recuperate lost histories and rehearse possible futures, but to be credible they must resonate with the realities of the here and now. As Louis Althusser shows, expressive culture has a semi-autonomous relationship with social structure that gives it the potential to serve both dominant and oppositional purposes at the same time.[12] Thus, there is no search for the perfect text of Black experience. Conflict increasingly becomes a valuable point of entry.

---

12. Louis Althusser, "Ideology and Ideological State Apparatuses," in *Lenin and Philosophy, and Other Essays*, trans. Ben Brewster (New York: Monthly Review Press, 2001).

Questions about language, meaning, and subjectivity have always accompanied African American literature and criticism. As Hortense Spillers notes, how can a Black subject speak a "truer word concerning myself" when the very grammar of American nationhood, culture, and politics has named and spoken blackness as the site of the other, of gender and sexual nonnormativity, of national threat, in short of necessary absence?[13] The language and names that accompany the Black subject in public U.S. discourse are examples of the "signifying property *plus*" that exceeds the logocentric model Derrida critiques and engages the extradiscursive formations that have long been objects of interest for Black scholars and writers.[14]

Given the realities of the color line, and the misrecognition of Black people that veiling entails, how do African Americans make their humanity known or have themselves recognized as citizens "without being cursed and spit upon by his fellows, without having the doors of Opportunity closed roughly in his face"?[15] Answering this question relates to the less familiar operation of Du Bois's veil. For working behind the scenes—and the not seen—of the veil, African Americans have turned segregation into congregation, looking to their institutions, spiritual and profane, to sustain them as a community. This sense of community and experience of congregation is not established solely because of racial oppression or out of a shared understanding of suffering. Frantz Fanon writes, "Black consciousness is immanent in its own eyes. I am not a potentiality of something, I am wholly what I am. I do not have to look for the universal. . . . My Negro consciousness does not hold itself out as lack. It *is*."[16] And this pertains to the scenes of intraracial relations, an invaluable source for considering Black ways of knowing, Black cosmologies, and Black experiences. As Claudia Tate[17] argues,

---

13. Hortense Spillers, "Mama's Baby, Papa's Maybe: An American Grammar Book," in *Black, White, and in Color*, 203.

14. Ibid.

15. W. E. B. Du Bois, *The Souls of Black Folk*, edited by Henry Louis Gates Jr. and Terri Hume Oliver (1903; New York: Bantam Books, 1989), 11.

16. Frantz Fanon, *Black Skin, White Masks* (1952; New York: Grove Press, 1967), 135.

17. Claudia Tate, *Psychoanalysis and Black Novels: Desire and the Protocols of Race* (New York: Oxford University Press, 1998), 10.

an approach to African American literature and literary criticism that only responds to Western concepts of race represses yearning, longing, and striving, making these aspects of Black subjectivity surplus, unrecognizable, and illegible. The veil, then, that shrouds intraracial dynamics and negotiations, can be seen as protective or what Edouard Glissant described as "opaque"[18] to the dominant White gaze. Signifying the finely tuned art of concealment, the veil also possesses a sexual connotation, cordoning off the personal, private, and intimate spaces of Black life. The space behind the veil, of Black intimate and even erotic experience, houses the opportunity for imagining a human condition not fully governed by, or accountable to, a White gaze. It refuses the demand to represent Black bodies solely in relationship to a discourse of historic claims on those bodies.

A shift in critical focus, then, to life behind the veil and thus to the lived complexities of intraracial dynamics forces us to think methodologically and epistemologically about Black intersubjectivity as a structure of being and as an approach to analyzing African American fiction. Such an analysis contests the racial grammar and language of representation itself. As James Baldwin observes, "For a black writer in this country to be born into the English language is to realize that the assumptions on which the language operates are his enemy."[19] Baldwin's many powerful essays regularly speak to the creative power and unique task of the Black writer and artist. For Black writers, commandeering the English language is part of the struggle of the Black radical tradition:

> The language forged by black people in this country, on this continent, as the choir just told you, got us from one place to another. We described the auction block. We described what it meant to be there. We survived what it meant to be torn from your mother, your father, your brother, your sister. We described it. We survived being described as mules, as having been put on earth only for the conve-

---

18. See Edouard Glissant, *Caribbean Discourse*, trans. J. Michael Dash (Charlottesville: University Press of Virginia, 1989).

19. James Baldwin, "On Language, Race, and the Black Writer," in *The Cross of Redemption: Uncollected Writings* (New York: Vintage Books, 2010), 140.

nience of white people. We survived having *nothing* belonging to us, not your mother, not your father, not your daughter, not your son. And we created the only language in this country.[20]

Described as a forging accomplished by Black people, language here is figured as undoing the chains of signification that uphold the auction block, slavery, and servitude. In this re-articulation, Black people are not simply the products of the language or its signifiers, but authors, literal forgers of them and their complex significations. Black subjectivity is therefore no longer produced by alienation from language, but from its artifaction, traversing a chain of signification that is not apprehended through the dominant terms of meaning and pursuits of truth. The play of language these authors unleash neither begins nor ends in the nothingness imposed by the logic of racial objecthood.

Baldwin suggests that the history and the praxis of the Black artist has been to create language, a new grammar, and thus a new subjectivity not rooted in the dominant terms of meaning and recognition. These artistic efforts are not about the celebration of marginality or the romanticization of otherness. Instead, Baldwin posits that in these descriptions of experience, be they of mother and father or of one's junkie cousin, accuracy of description of difficult conditions is a way to begin to overcome them. Further, these descriptions are not committed to, or created to, reveal a truth. In the essay "Of the Sorrow Songs: The Cross of Redemption," Baldwin challenges the authority of claims to truth. He begins with a falsehood:

July 29, 1979
I will let the date stand: but it is a false date. My typewriter has been silent since July 6th, and the piece of paper I placed in the typewriter on that day has been blank until this hour.

July 29th was—is—my baby sister's birthday. She is now thirty-six years old, is married to a beautiful cat, and they have a small son, my nephew, one of my many nephews. My baby sister was born on the day our father died: and I could not but wonder what she, or our

---

20. James Baldwin, "Black English: A Dishonest Argument," in ibid., 156.

> father, or her son, my nephew, could possibly make of this compelling investigation of our lives.
>
> It is compelling indeed, like the nightmare called history: and compelling because the author is as precise as he is deluded.[21]

The distinction brings us to that between political and creative realms, the former that demands unity, the latter that is shaped by conflict. There has always been an uneasy but necessary relationship between Black literary culture and Black politics. The struggle Baldwin articulates is to bring White America and those invested in whiteness to see the relationship between the denial of racism and how that denial informs the direction of Black politics. In other words, Black inclusion into the polity, into civil society, and into equality has required wresting some form of recognition from White people. The refusal of such recognition, whether that comes in the form of resistance to recognition or renegotiation of its terms, characterizes the opposition to Black movements for racial justice and the ongoing work of struggle.

It is vital to oppose White supremacy, but disastrous to become totally defined by it. Black authors cannot let Black people become only the mirror image needed by White supremacists. It falls to Black literary culture and Black aesthetics to produce a new grammar and language that is not calibrated solely by White refusal, but rather useful to a Black radical tradition that persists because of such misrecognition. The ongoing struggle found in the political sphere refracts the persistent representation of intraracial conflict and forms of representation that resist simple decoding through the dominant terms for recognizing humanity and truth. Although the representation of conflict seems to run counter to the political demand for unity, the depictions of intimate, intraracial conflict operate in one of the most challenging sites for constituting Black subjectivity by traversing the very language set up for Black illegibility and misrecognition. Instead, the literature consistently seeks escape from language's—and thus politics'—own presumptions. It emphasizes

---

21. James Baldwin, "Of the Sorrow Songs: The Cross of Redemption," in ibid., 145.

the process of creation rather than reaction. It conflicts with those seeking recognition on dominant terms imagining that coherence and unity will inevitably lead to transcendence. It recognizes that the process of becoming is not static.

The term *intimate antagonisms* emphasizes conflict on the microscale of interpersonal relations. Examinations of intimacy[22] by cultural studies scholars tend to emphasize the role of the state in designating and controlling public and private spaces, bodies, and relations. Yet private interactions have public causes and consequences. These conflicts take place in the context of incessant demands for a unity that looks like uniformity, for an identity that cruelly insists people be identical. The exercise of racial subordination, including the group-differentiated subjection to premature death[23] along with de facto and de jure forms of segregation, have compelled intraracial identification and congregation. Forced communion and shared suffering, however, do not automatically result in communal cohesion and harmony. Moreover, structural forces of subordination (labor discrimination, unequal housing, mass incarceration, welfare policies) have long targeted Black intimate life for confinement and control. Intimate vulnerabilities, as Candace Jenkins explains, point out the impediments to full participation in the U.S. polity, which bestows "membership in America's 'civilized' sociopolitical world, with all the respectability and assumed normalcy such membership would entail." The realm of the intimate represents a key arena within which Black people struggle both to be full citizens and "to be understood as such."[24]

Black intimate life is also a potential location for the expression of vulnerability and desire, and a place for cultivating creative visions of love and liberation. In her examination of Lorraine Hansberry's play *A Raisin in the Sun,* Tricia Rose turns to Black literary produc-

---

22. Psychology is the other field most concerned with definitions, descriptions, and analyses of intimacy. Scholars of intimacy emerging from psychology tend to focus on nuclear familial relations with an emphasis on understanding or enhancing those bonds.

23. See Ruth Wilson Gilmore, *Golden Gulag: Prisons, Surplus, Crisis, and Opposition in Globalizing California* (Berkeley: University of California Press, 2007).

24. Candace Jenkins, *Private Lives, Proper Relations: Regulating Black Intimacy* (Minneapolis: University of Minnesota Press, 2007), 3, 4.

tion specifically to develop her concept of "(inter)personal justice."[25] Attending to the "crucial role of intimate relationships and community formations in producing or suffocating social justice movements or other forms of radical resistance," interpersonal justice brings together analyses of structural forms of inequality and interpersonal dynamics.[26] Emphasis on the private nature of intimate antagonisms consciously ignores the ways that the private/public divide has never been available to Black people. Labor outside the home as cooks, butlers, chauffeurs, gardeners, and nannies often took place in White people's domestic spaces, whereas the private realm of the Black home has always been a site of White surveillance and supervision. Scenes of domestic disputes and communal conflicts have clear connections to public struggles for Black liberation and justice. Portrayals of conflict, tensions, or even abuses form part of that process of community-building and imagining racial community. Analyses of intimate antagonisms show us how African American literary texts continue to be important spaces for examining Black social consciousness about the meaning of resistance. Intimate antagonisms reveal something that the political sphere writ large does not fully capture. Within intimate spaces and relations, the wounds are more present than in the political narratives of Black social movements. Intimate antagonisms are the site where the most hurtful pains are negotiated—and literature has a particular affinity for revealing those wounds and possibilities precisely because they exceed the boundaries of what is considered "sayable" and knowable about Black social life. Intimate antagonisms and the trope of the intraracial refuse the reduction of Black literature to a response to White hegemony. Rather, this literature produces a vision of Black social life wherein intimacy and antagonism are not oppositional to each other but coexist and crosscut each other. Black literature reveals an intellectual modality whereby intimacy and antagonism are not only

---

25. Tricia Rose, "Hansberry's *A Raisin in the Sun* and the 'Illegible' Politics of (Inter)personal Justice," *Kalfou* 1.1 (Spring 2014): 27–60.
26. Ibid., 33.

represented but also productive sites of experimentation where we imagine and try to speak our own language.

•

With a focus on intraracial conflicts and intimate antagonisms, this book scrutinizes and challenges the typical three *R*s of Black literary studies: respectability, recognition, and resistance. Representations of intimate antagonisms in Black literature trouble the foundations of respectability. They refuse dominant conceptions of gender, sexual, and cultural normativity, and understand intimacy itself as countercultural. Moreover, in highlighting representations of Black interpersonal relations, my work challenges the assumption that public and private are separate and incommensurable spheres. It offers a framework for literary and social critique that recognizes how the interpenetration of these spheres peculiarly affects Black lives and formulations of Black subjectivities. Bringing a focus on intimate antagonisms into engagement with the Black radical tradition produces an alternative model for reading. It offers a Black radical methodology for engaging Black literature that draws on Rose's conception of (inter)personal justice as "politically generative work that goes on in relational, private spaces and social interactions" and "*the development of political consciousness that goes on within these interpersonal spaces.*"[27] Holding the two together helps transform Black literature into a public forum that finally does not pit Black progress against Black community. It allows Black literature to be expressive and expansive of the multiply vexed ways that Black people love.

Black Love, Black Hate is divided into four chapters that cover four periods of Black sociopolitical activity: the Great Black Migration, the civil rights movement, the Black Power and Black feminist movements, and the post–civil rights and Obama eras. To illustrate the pervasiveness and critical significance of intimate antagonisms in African American fiction, each chapter examines a range of texts that depict intracommunal conflicts emerging in Black literature during key moments of Black struggles for racial justice.

---

27. Rose, "Hansberry's *A Raisin in the Sun*," 33.

Chapter 1 analyzes African American literature emerging out of the experiences of Black people's urban migrations to and habitation in U.S. cities. I argue that the upheavals associated with the processes of migration create the conditions of possibility for the emergence of intimate antagonisms in African American literature. I examine New Negro Renaissance representations of tensions in the too-close quarters of the segregated North and South. Whereas most scholars writing about the literature of this era focus on the color line as determinant of racial identity, I show how these texts always point to life behind the veil or, as Hurston phrases it, Black life "beneath the bed-clothes." In particular, I explore the many representations of confinement and flight in works by Negro Renaissance artists as they negotiate the meaning of community given the segregated and overcrowded quarters of emergent "Bronzevilles" and other Black urban spaces. To Farrah Jasmine Griffin's masterful description of the "migration narrative"[28] I add the specific focus on lines of flight evident in the works of canonical writers Nella Larsen, Zora Neale Hurston, and Wallace Thurman. Their writings place "black spatiality" and "black intimacy" in dialogue with the articulation of New Negro theories of Black cultural politics.

Chapter 2 examines the seemingly paradoxical emphasis on Black interiority in literature produced during the apex of the civil rights movement. Why, during this era of explicit racial challenges to White supremacy, does African American literature insist on representations of Black inner life? My claim is that solidarity runs counter to intimacy and sexual diversity, and that Black literary emphasis on this phenomenon goes beyond "high modernism" to contest Black heteronormativity. In dialogue with and against traditional historiographies of African American literature, I argue that civil rights agendas and their focus on Black political subjectivity exist in sharp contrast to Black literary portrayals of Black interiority. From Ralph Ellison's *Invisible Man* (1952) to James Baldwin's *Go Tell It on the Mountain* (1953) and Gwendolyn Brooks's *Maud Martha* (1953), the complex structure of the Black psyche finds sustained attention

---

28. Farrah Jasmine Griffin, *Who Set You Flowin'?: The African American Migration Narrative, Race and American Culture* (New York: Oxford University Press, 1996).

unmatched since Du Bois's formulation of double consciousness and its singular depiction in Jean Toomer's *Cane* (1923). These novels, including Chester Hime's *If He Hollers Let Him Go* (1945) and *Lonely Crusade* (1947), emphasize the challenges inherent in recognizing Black racial, gendered, and sexual identities. Their writings address the conflict between what Baldwin describes as the "wishful-shameful fantasies" that White supremacist American culture imposes on Black people, and Black people's negotiations of that imposition with themselves and with each other.

Chapter 3 addresses how the intergenerational legacies of and responses to gendered racism shape depictions of private life and intimate desire. While intimate antagonisms between Black men and women about the racial and gendered hierarchy do not begin in the late 1960s, the intensification of such painful clashes compel the analysis of the complex visions of struggle that Black Power and Black Feminist mobilizations produce. Perhaps no other epoch unleashes such a range of intracommunal tensions as this era, which is also the period of emergence for the neo-slave narrative. As I argue, depictions of intraracial sexual violence reference what Hortense Spillers calls the "originating metaphors of captivity and mutilation" that defined the condition of the enslaved in the United States. Black feminists contend that slavery and its attendant dispossessions separated Black womanhood from normative femininity and assigned Black women a central role in determining raced and gendered identities by contrast. If established definitions of patriarchal authority include both access to and protection over women's bodies, how do we deal with the legacies of the central role of rape in the antebellum plantation system? The acknowledgment of such abuse would expose the relationship between patriarchy, White supremacy, and sexual violence. Because Black Power discourses *also* made claims to Black patriarchy as a means to redress the disempowering and therefore emasculating effects of racism, their demands sought the redemption of Black manhood without posing a sufficient challenge to the principles of patriarchy that remain linked to traditional definitions of U.S. citizenship. What became a demand for political recognition at the height of civil rights and Black Power activities attached Black manhood to political and racial justice. Although this particular history of the Black Power era is well traversed, my analysis examines how this intraracial discord helped shape the neo-slave narrative in African American fiction. The emergence of Black feminism from Black women's involvement in the civil rights and Black Power movements positioned Black feminist criticism centrally in the examination of intraracial antagonisms. In their refusal of Black women's experiences with racism, the dominant narratives of slavery threatened racial justice, especially in a moment of Black insurgency. The chapter analyzes novels by Gayl Jones, Margaret Walker, and Toni Morrison.

Chapter 4 brings my analysis to contemporary debates about whether class relations take precedence over race in color-blind conceptions of oppression. The chapter examines the shifting terrain of discourses on race and class in the post–civil rights eras and the ways that depictions of intraracial class conflict provide grounds for rethinking the meaning of racial progress, resistance, and community in the present. One cannot overstate the number of representations of intimate antagonisms resulting from economic stratification among African Americans after the gains achieved from civil rights and feminist movement victories. Nonetheless, ongoing social concerns related to the prison industrial complex, the shrinking welfare state, and persistent poverty also produce communal fractures. The emphases on "hard work" and self-reliance reinvigorate "bootstrap" politics that elevate the class interests of Black people considered "exceptional" over those dismissed as "disposable." This chapter argues that post–civil rights African American literature does not feature the triumph of class over race. Instead, contemporary Black writers, even those associated with "post Soul" aestheticism (Andrea Lee, Trey Ellis, Paul Beatty), popular cultural genres (gangsta literature, urban romance, etc.), and canonical texts (John Edgar Wideman, Colson Whitehead, Alice Randall) continually depict linked fates that connect middle-class and working-class African Americans. Education, as a primary means to attain class mobility in U.S. society, figures prominently for the elaboration of the trope of the intraracial. The thwarted promise of education as a path to assimilation or social transformation forces an intraracial dialogue about race, class, and liberation in post–civil rights Black literature.

Finally, *Black Love, Black Hate* concludes with a discussion of the role of cultural expression, especially literature, in the face of current multiculturalist and antiracist discourses. Attention to intraracial dynamics and negotiations problematizes the critique of ethnic literatures as sources for teaching White people about racial difference and racial tolerance. Instead, a critical engagement with the representations of intraracial conflict demands that readers consider the interface between poetics and politics in the construction of textual and ideological spaces for Black community deliberation and debate.

I engage with the Movement for Black Lives in response to police murder and the general U.S. disregard for Black existence demonstrated in repeated grand jury decisions that legitimate law enforcement officers in their destruction of Black lives. Public discussions of these issues raise questions about intraracial violence and conflict as a way of concealing the state's power over life and death. This discussion urges on readers the need to challenge the dominant discourse of Black-on-Black violence for its reification of Black pathology, but at the same time signals the importance of creating spaces for confronting intraracial antagonisms that sometimes lead to exploitation, brutality, and even death. Our inability to engage with these concerns capitulates to the dominant society's refusals of Black agency. The Black queer politics of the blacklivesmatters' founders and mission signal the evolution and ongoing significance of intimate antagonisms of past and present eras. Engaging them helps construct antiracist epistemologies grounded in the Black radical tradition. While the depictions that animate this project emerge from literature, they remain connected to broader political, social, economic, and cultural concerns.

CHAPTER 1

The Public Space of Intimate Antagonisms

Black Intimacy and Opposition to Jim Crow

> *There is no privacy in an African village. Loves, fights, possessions are, to misquote Woodrow Wilson, "Open disagreements openly arrived at." The community is given the benefit of a good fight as well as a good wedding. An audience is a necessary part of any drama. We merely go with nature rather than against it.*
>
> —Zora Neale Hurston,
> "Characteristics of Negro Expression"

IN "CHARACTERISTICS of Negro Expression"[1] (1934) Zora Neale Hurston presents a brief but generative discussion of the art and performance of intraracial conflict in the cramped quarters Black folks are forced to occupy under legal, racial segregation. "Jim Crow," the popular reference to the U.S. epoch of racial apartheid, produced policies and practices for maintaining racial segregation and disenfranchisement that depended upon a violent culture of segregation.[2] Painful conditions sometimes spur creativity. "Discord is more natural than accord," she states; "humanity places premiums on all things necessary to its well-being, and a valiant and good fighter is valuable

---

1. Cited parenthetically throughout.
2. On the culture of segregation, see for examples, Ida B. Wells, *Crusade for Justice: The Autobiography of Ida B. Wells* (Chicago: University of Chicago Press, 1970); Elizabeth Grace Hale, *Making Whiteness: The Culture of Segregation in the South, 1890–1940* (New York: Pantheon Books, 1998); and William H. Chafe, *Remembering Jim Crow: African Americans Tell About Life in the Segregated South* (New York: New Press, 2001).

in any community" (60). Hurston's references to fighting and "warfare" acknowledge the community's subjection to racist terror during the Jim Crow period. Such skill in combat demands exhibition: "hence the holding of all quarrels and fights in the open" (61). Intraracial drama is a product of the aesthetic negotiation of Jim Crow confinement. "Love-making and fighting in all their branches are high arts," Hurston proclaims, for "other things are arts among other groups where they brag about their proficiency just as brazenly as we do about these things that others consider matters for conversation behind closed doors" (ibid.).

Hurston's essay emerged at a critical conjuncture in Black political and literary history. Scholars of the New Negro era, then and now, emphasize the importance of divorcing Black people from the images and caricatures of African descendants as docile, shufflin', and uncultured. The assertion of the emergence of a "New Negro" in the early twentieth century sought to portray Black Americans as culturally, intellectually, and morally prepared to defend their rights to civil and civilized inclusion. New Negro activities included emphasizing cultural production as foundational to racial uplift.[3] That era's deep investment in Black letters, art, and performance as bases for demonstrating Black value and readiness for inclusion in U.S. society continues to impact the demands we place on Black American cultural expression.

These New Negro sentiments about the value of cultural achievement cannot be understood apart from the profound significance of the Great Black Migration on the geographical, political, and identitarian shifts among Black peoples during the early twentieth century. The mass movement of Black Americans from rural to Southern and Northern urban areas in the industrializing United States is an example of Black people's exercise of agency and democracy as citizens despite and in opposition to the systematic refusal of their civil rights. The Great Black Migration produced a synergy with the Negro Renaissance that celebrated Black achievement in cultural

---

3. For an analysis of the debates over cultural production and racial uplift, see Paul Allen Anderson, *Deep River: Music and Memory in Harlem Renaissance Thought* (Durham: Duke University Press, 2001).

forms otherwise dominated by White writers and artists, and fueled the desire for Black people to take advantage of the opportunities in the growing audiences for their creative wares.[4] The Negro Renaissance was a beacon and symbol of the hope and possibility to transform dominant ideologies of Black inferiority and to contest the racist spatial arrangements and culture of Jim Crow segregation. In this way, the Negro Renaissance was another "pull" factor[5] drawing Black migrants to urban areas and life *even as* those literary representations regularly featured scenes of intraracial antagonism.

Hurston comments on the very public nature of intraracial conflicts. In fact, her description establishes equivalence between real intraracial antagonism and its artistic representation. The quarrels and couplings she describes require both performers and an audience. The performance of open disagreements rises to the level of art with all the stylistic contrivances that artistic creation entails. The all-permeating drama of Negro life emerges from intimate antagonisms in the racially segregated spaces of African American life. The aesthetic of conflict so characteristic of Black art emerges from Black folks' interactions, experiences, frustrations, desires, talents, and passions. From the juke joint to the sanctified church, Hurston's description of what characterizes Black cultural expression organizes itself around the intraracial dynamics of Black life given the culture of segregation. Many New Negro Renaissance artists address a similar concern: How do Black people convert segregation into congregation? And simultaneously, how do the issues of segregation and migration find expression in respective representations of confinement and flight intraracially?

The contexts of racial segregation and Black migration produce representations of intraracial confinement and flight within African American literature that challenge the presumption of homogeneity as the basis for collectivity. Sentiments of confinement and the desire for flight are responses to Jim Crow segregation and the terror of de facto lynch laws. It would be incorrect, however, to presume

---

4. Nathan Irvin Huggins, *Harlem Renaissance* (New York: Oxford University Press, 1971).

5. See Carole Marks, *Farewell—We're Good and Gone: The Great Black Migration* (Bloomington: Indiana University Press, 1989).

that these intraracial conflicts only offer release valves for the suppressed rage, frustration, and humiliation experienced at the color line. The representations of confinement and flight examined in this chapter through readings of Hurston's, Wallace Thurman's, and Nella Larsen's respective novels do not simply react to anti-Black racism and exclusion. There is another side to the exposure of the messiness that unfolds scandalously in the most intimate quarters of Black life in industrializing American cities.

Intraracial debates over the terms of collectivity and the modalities for uplift become repeated tropes in the depiction of intraracial and intimate antagonisms in New Negro literature. Flight emerges as a form of protest and a process of self-discovery as it illuminates alternative bases for communal cohesion. Mobility, therefore, shapes an aesthetic of rebellion, rupture, and transformation. The realities of migration become an aesthetic of movement in the re-presentation of intimate antagonisms—antagonisms that provoke intraracial debate about the meanings of race and space, and struggle between being and community.

INTIMATE ANTAGONISMS AND THE BLACK MIGRATION NARRATIVE

It was hard to love a woman that always made you feel so wishful.

—Zora Neale Hurston, *Their Eyes Were Watching God*

Janie Crawford, one of Hurston's most memorable fictional protagonists, for example, negotiates the drama of Negro life and the absence of privacy in *Their Eyes Were Watching God*.[6] The narrative is propelled by Janie's negotiation of intimate antagonisms in three romantic relationships with Logan Killicks, Jody Starks, and Tea Cake. In the segregated southern communities she negotiates, and in the process narrates, the terms of communal belonging and personal free-

---

6. Zora Neale Hurston, *Their Eyes Were Watching God* (Philadelphia: Lippincott, 1937). Cited parenthetically throughout.

dom, as well as the intraracial debates over confinement and escape. Her involvement with each suitor provokes the confinement/flight dialectic through intraracial, intimate antagonisms. Overall, Janie's portrayal of her intimate experiences, confinement, and flight to her friend Phoebe forms *Their Eyes Were Watching God*. The title thus suggests a communal gathering around Janie's intimate and often antagonistic experiences and her narration of them.

The novel structures the narrative of Janie's life around two gendered images: ships and a tree. These two organizing figures represent the intraracial tension in the confinement/flight dialectic that the narrative develops. "Ships at a distance have every man's wish on board," the omniscient narrator declares at the novel's opening (1). These ships are vessels of masculine desire that sometimes "come in with the tide," but more often pursue the horizon "never out of sight, never landing until the Watcher turns his eyes away in resignation, his dreams mocked to death by Time" (1). The narrator characterizes this endless, watching, waiting, and hoping with the "life of men," not the universal "man." The men referred to here are the Black males who make up the community in which Janie's narrative unfolds. The following paragraph further undercuts the universalist view of ships, movement, desire, and time. "Now, women forget all those things they don't want to remember, and remember everything they don't want to forget," the narrator offers as a way of introducing the readers to a conflicting and feminized viewpoint about wishes, frustration, and memory (ibid.). For women, the narrator asserts, "the dream is the truth" and the site from which women act (ibid.). The conflicting gendered point of view is the beginning of the novel and the site from which Janie comes "back from burying the dead" (ibid.). For her, the sudden dead with their "eyes flung wide open in judgment" marks her entry into the narrative, and her re-entry to the community. With their day labors, toils, and subordination behind them, this community of working-class Black women and men feel "powerful and human" in the absence of the "sun and the bossman" (ibid.). Yet in the tongues, ears, and eyes they take back from the degradations of servile labor, they sit in judgment upon seeing Janie, the woman who "made them remember the envy they had stored up from other times" (2).

Their Eyes Were Watching God opens by situating Black men's and women's responses to deferred dreams and thwarted wishes within the context of Black subordination and exploitation. Even still, the people of Janie's community reserve their hostilities for the woman who seems to embody or provoke the memories of their unfulfilled wishes:

> The men noticed her firm buttocks like she had grape fruits in her hip pockets; the great rope of black hair swinging to her waist and unraveling in the wind like a plume; then her pugnacious breasts trying to bore holes in her shirt. They, the men, were saving with the mind what they lost with the eye. The women took the faded shirt and muddy overalls and laid them away for remembrance. It was a weapon against her strength and if it turned out of no significance, still it was a hope that she might fall to their level some day. (2)

This early passage from the novel appropriates Jim Crow images to characterize intraracial antagonisms. The men's piercing and desirous gaze seizes upon the fertility of Janie's hips, described in comparison to plump grape fruits. Her long black hair, however, arrests this image of fecundity, for it swings like a rope and unravels like a plume. Although plume can refer to an ornamental feather symbolizing status or to the emission of rising smoke, the term used to describe Janie's attraction checks masculine authority over her body. Even "her pugnacious breasts" bore holes in her shirt, while her overall appearance forces men to save "with the mind what they lost with the eye." The men's wish, projected onto Janie's body, is for the aggressiveness and status that her movement seems to disclose. Janie's mobility, in other words, embodies the masculine desire and mobility that lynching sought to obstruct. In the Black men's eyes, Janie represents the elusiveness of ships at a distance and the reminder of the mocking of dreams. The ostensible traits for violently controlling Black masculinity come to rest on the characterization of Janie's body. In other words, the control over and representation of Black mobility, bodies, and desire are redefined intraracially in the novel according to their meaning for Black women and men.

The women, trained in what to remember and forget, hold on to Janie's shabby appearance. They hold this image as a "weapon against her strength" revealed in the worn look of adventure and mobility that her faded shirt and muddy overalls signify. The hope they reserve is that she too will "fall to their level," that her spirit and body will come under confinement. Unlike the men, the women's resentments over the feelings of confinement find expression in Janie's return, the "hope she might fall to their level some day" (2). The vision of intraracial community that the novel opens with animates conceptions of envy and distrust rather than cohesion and belonging. Hurston's notion of the absence of the concept of privacy further characterizes her neighbors' gossip:

> What she doin coming back here in dem overhalls? Can't she find no dress to put on?—where's dat blue satin dress she left here in?— What dat ole forty year ole 'oman doin' wid her hair swingin' down her back lak some young gal?—Where she left dat young lad of a boy she went off here wid?—Thought she was going to marry?—Where he left *her*? (2)

The novel discloses the narrative of Janie's experiences with mobility at the outset, but through the mocking voices of the other Black women and men confined to a segregated space. These voices make up the "'porch' that couldn't talk for looking" at Janie's walk. The looking that occupies the community's imagination and resentment, however, also indicates their identification with Janie, an identification that compels their gaze and simultaneously provokes their anxiety. There is something irresistible in her appearance that garners the "mass cruelty" of the women and men who receive her. The community's wish for ships and nagging memory of something they long to forget are intertwined in the perception of Janie's escape from the community and her return to their location of frustrated confinement.

The other image within the dialectic of confinement and escape is the tree, a figure existing in contention with the ships. Janie sees "her life like a great tree in leaf with the things suffered, things enjoyed, things done and undone. Dawn and doom was in the branches" (8). Stretched out beneath a pear tree listening to the birds and the bees, Janie recalls her sexual awakening and learns the history of her family's sexual abuse. Janie is the product of interracial rape (as was her mother before her). She learns the history of sexual abuse in her female family line from her grandmother, whose daughter, the result of sexual relations with a member of the plantation-owning family, is born on the eve of Emancipation. The history of sexual violence interrupts the promise of Emancipation and engenders a wound that Black women bear. The consequences of that wound manifest in the possibilities for intraracial intimacies (which we will see again in chapter 3). The novel chronicles Janie's experiences of domestic abuse from African American husbands and lovers, and the internalization of racialized and gendered violence within the southern Black community. "You know," her grandmother confides, "us colored folks is branches without roots and that makes things come round in queer ways" (15). Her grandmother's lesson is for Janie to resist the feelings of defeat and confinement: "But nothing can't stop you from wishin'. You can't beat nobody down so low till you can rob 'em of they will" (15). Janie's ability to continue wishing even as she remembers the experiences of intimate pain structures the remainder of the novel.

Logan Killicks becomes Janie's first husband after her grandmother ("Nanny") arranges the marriage for Janie's economic security. Nevertheless, Janie's marriage to Logan contains none of the sweetness and wonder of the pear tree. With her first dream of love dead, "she became a woman" and halfheartedly accustoms herself to the kitchen duties Logan requires to maintain his sixty acres (24). "Ah'll take holt uh dat ax and come in dere and kill yuh! You better dry up in dere! Ah'm too honest and hard-workin' for anybody in yo' family, dat's de reason you don't want me!" Logan half sobs and half cries to Janie (30). His harsh words sting Janie and solidify her resolve to leave Logan with Joe Starks, whom she subsequently marries.

Killicks offers Janie a life of duty, toil, sweat, and servitude, while those around her remind her of her good fortune: "If you don't want him, you sho oughta. Heah you is wid de onliest organ in town, amongst colored folks, in yo' parlor. Got a house bought and paid for and sixty acres uh land right on de big road . . . Lawd have mussy! Dat's de very prong all us black women gits hung on. Dis love!" (22). In *Their Eyes Were Watching God,* Logan aligns with a generation content to hold their heads to the plow. Janie is more of a helper rather than a helpmeet. Lacking companionship and connection, their marriage becomes an exercise in feminine submission to a vision of toil and labor that provides sustenance and survival without passion. This rural vision of Black life and survival is nonetheless rooted in intraracial conflict, as Logan's angry comments about Janie's family and his respectability reveal.

Janie's rejection of and departure from marriage with Killicks also challenges the vision of racial uplift through labor and accommodation as espoused by Booker T. Washington. Washington, known for the creation of the Tuskegee Normal and Industrial Institute and his autobiography *Up from Slavery* (1901), championed the view that education and productive labor could engender racial uplift and progress despite the ongoing law and rule of segregation. In addition to his refusal to indict White racism for the conditions Black southerners face, Washington's personal narrative sacrifices personality and emotion in order to summon support for Black autonomy, education, and uplift. Similarly, Logan Killicks attempts to adjust Janie to the plow as a form of racial improvement through marriage and labor: "Heah, Ah just as good as take you out de white folks' kitchen and set you down on yo' royal diasticutis and you take and low-rate me!" (30). Logan perceives her labor on his farm as an elevation from the confines of domestic labor otherwise available to Black women. Still, Janie rejects a vision of marriage, intimacy, and communion based on the utilitarian notion of industriousness seeking to prop up a tentative sense of pride and independence. Hurston's narrative provides a critique of racial uplift politics through Janie's movement in and through intimate conflicts and relations.

In contrast to Logan Killicks's emphasis on humbled labor as the basis of racial pride, Joe Starks provides Janie with a New Negro sensibility. Once she leaves Logan, she travels with Starks by hired rig, train, and buggy to the "colored town" where he plans to remake himself along with the community. "Ah figgers we all needs uh store in uh big hurry. . . . Yeah, uh store right heah in town wid everything in it you needs. 'Tain't uh bit uh use in everybody proagin' way over tuh Maitland tuh buy uh little meal and flour when they could get it right heah," Starks proclaims to the gathered Eatonville townspeople (37). With lightning speed, they form a committee to discuss the town's development, and with "Jody doing all the talking" they decide to designate a day to form roads, drum up citizens to move to Eatonville, and begin to see new families buying lots and moving into the town (38). Economic mobility, however, proves to bifurcate the vision of racial community again.

Joe Starks's store becomes a center of commerce and politics. This new public space is also the launching pad for Starks's distinction from Killicks: "Ah means tuh put mah hands tuh de plow heah, and strain every nerve tuh make dis our town de metropolis uh de state" (40). With his hands to the plow over the fifty acres that make up Eatonville, Starks sets into motion a new vision of community that differs in scale from Killicks's version of individualized uplift and conformist survival. Instead, Starks implements a politico-economic vision of Black uplift, but one that remains confined to a vision of patriarchal respectability and economic impersonality. When Janie is asked to publicly address the community, Joe intercedes: "Thank yuh fuh yo' compliments, but mah wife don't know nothin' 'bout no speech-makin.' Ah never married her for nothin' lak dat. She's uh woman and her place is in de home" (40–41). His newly established dignity enables him to think and plan out loud "unconscious of her thoughts" (41).

But the novel itself is organized around Janie's thoughts and perspectives. The narrative issues from Janie's overarching conversation with her dear friend Phoebe, so despite the fact that an omniscient narrator arranges the novel's plot and dialogue, Janie remains the indirect focalizer of *Their Eyes Were Watching God*. It is from her perspective, therefore, that the reader apprehends the intraracial fragmentation and intimate antagonisms that threaten communal cohesion in Eatonville. "The town had a basketful of feelings good and bad about Joe's positions and possessions, but none had the temerity to challenge him. They bowed down to him rather, because he was all of these things, and then again he was all of these things because the town bowed down" (47).

The Black public that Joe presides over, whether in politics, business, or his storefront, create spaces to stage dissenting voices. On the one hand, the banter, exchange, and gathering in these spaces provide an escape from the degradations of poverty and confinement of limited opportunities. On the other hand, intraracial controls over public speech and participation establish new forms of constraint within a community attempting to create and define itself. The spaces may produce a town-hall forum, but one key topic is over who is sanctioned to represent the community. If the Black spatial imaginary refers to socially shared understandings of public space and the power to create new opportunities and life chances, then Eatonville's intraracial politics indicate the gendered function of intimate antagonisms involved in determining such collective meaning.

The intimate crisis between Joe and Janie symbolizes intraracial conflict over community formation and cohesion. As Claudia Tate argues, the "domestic ideation of black political desire in African-American literature" often utilized the portrayal of Black intimate life as a means to consider Black politics.[7] During the Negro Renaissance however, repeated scenes of domestic tragedy, parody, and satire challenge the idealized scenes of domesticity in post-Reconstruction era literature.[8] While contesting inequality with regard to race and gender generated a protest aesthetic,[9] Negro Renaissance narratives of intimate antagonisms demonstrates how Black political desire also concerns the textures and complexities of Black life. Janie gains the strength of her own voice as Joe's health decreases.

The weakening of Joe's physical health parallels the fragmentation of his relationship to Janie despite the growth of his store's commerce and Eatonville's population. "The more people in [the store] the more ridicule he poured over her body to point attention away from his own" (74). Joe's ill health is indicative of dis-ease in his vision of community and related Black masculinist forms of dignity. Instead of maintaining the appearance of race leader and entrepreneur, his declining health reveals his weakness and vulnerability. Janie exposes

---

7. Claudia Tate, *Domestic Allegories of Political Desire: The Black Heroine's Text at the Turn of the Century* (New York: Oxford University Press, 1992), 14–15.

8. Ibid., 15.

9. Ibid., 17.

Starks's insults as deflections from his own emasculation: "But Ah'm uh woman every inch of me, and Ah know it. Dat's uh whole lot more'n *you* kin say. You big-bellies round here and put out a lot of brag, but 'tain't nothin' to it but yo' big voice. Humph! Talkin' 'bout *me* lookin' old! When you pull down yo' britches, you look lak de change uh life" (75). Robbed of what the narrator describes as the "illusion of irresistible maleness that all men cherish," Joe strikes "Janie with all his might and drove her from the store" (75, 76).

Their fight targets the fragility of her femininity and of his masculinity. It also evokes Black men's visions of ships and Black women's association with trees that open the novel. Janie's attempt to hold her ground roots her in a position wherein her voice's authority threatens Joe in the place where he seeks power. His masculine mobility brings him to Eatonville, where he establishes himself as a leader, entrepreneur, and husband. Janie's insult targets Joe beneath his "britches" and rejects him in his masculinity. The public refusal of Black phallic power in this context challenges the masculine presumption of the community's very formation. Branding Janie old and therefore no longer desirable robs her of the most basic way women are valued as sexually viable objects for men: "Nobody in heah ain't lookin' for no wife outa yuh. Old as you is" (75). For Black women, however, such an insult also conjures what those women would seek to forget: the history of sexual exploitation that accompanies Black women's valuation as women and their simultaneous subjection to sexual violence.

This pivotal scene in the deterioration of the Stark marriage portrays Janie and Joe as witness to and symbols of each other's shortcomings. Talking "under people's clothes," Joe and Janie's fight emerges from their public unveiling (ibid.). Although the bitter fight between the couple provides the townspeople the benefit of a good fight, Janie's words and Joe's fist rupture the narrative of mobility. Their verbal and physical assault takes place in the context of the commercial success of Starks's store. Eatonville finds itself enjoying population and infrastructural growth. Even so, the couple's intimate antagonism and their verbal denuding point to fractures within the community despite the process of racial uplift. Racial uplift ideology[10] most often references Black elite's investment in class mobility and respectable behavior. The town's economic development and Stark's emphasis on gender normativity and class differentiation produces intraracial hierarchies even as Eatonville and his store prosper. As Kevin Gaines argues, elite Black people depended upon "white political and business elites in the pursuit of race progress," relying on powerful White people who asserted control over poor Black and White labor.[11] The audience for Joe and Janie's fight includes those working-class Black people who are also left out of Starks's vision of racial uplift. Class and gender divisions emerge, and Eatonville becomes a final resting place. Such a version of community impedes a more expansive view of mobility and produces flight as a necessity from the confinement that such a stifling vision of collectivity contains.

Only six pages separate the couple's conflict and Joe (Jody) Starks's death. Similar to her original encounter with Joe, Tea Cake, a new love interest, comes into her life with mystery and a narrative: "She knew she didn't know his name, but he looked familiar. 'Good evenin', Mis' Starks,' he said with a sly grin as if they had a good joke together. She was in favor of the story that was making him laugh before she even heard it" (90). If Logan Killicks alludes to the Old Negro spirit and Joe Starks to the New, Tea Cake symbolizes the romanticization of the new Black South. Unlike Killicks and Starks, Tea Cake offers Janie no promise of stability or of conventional romance.

Happy to be away from Eatonville, but saddened by Tea Cake's stealth departure from their bed with her money in tow, Janie awakens to the sound of "somebody playing a guitar outside her door. Played right smart while. It sounded lovely too. But it was sad to hear it feeling blue like Janie was. Then whoever it was started to singing 'Ring de bells of mercy. Called de sinner man home.' Her heart all but smothered her. 'Tea Cake, is dat you?'" (115). Tea Cake brings with him his own dreams of flight and mobility. He proclaims

---

10. See Kevin Gaines, *Uplifting the Race*.
11. Ibid., xiv.

himself "one uh de best gamblers God ever made," but he joins his dice and cards with a switchblade knife (119). His version of masculine mobility is a form of what Toni Morrison describes as dangerous freedom.[12] This version of freedom disregards the demands of intimate connections (and community ones) in order to maintain a sense of physical and emotional mobility. Living dangerously free shrugs at normativity and the law. Janie's sense of mobility within the vision of trees, birds, and desire does not fully align with Tea Cake's individualism and rugged masculinity. Instead he remains untethered and dangerously so. Yet his unconventionality is not, as other scholars[13] suggest, problematic for its refusal of dominant forms of normativity through traditional marriage, patriarchy, and domestic confinement. Nonetheless, such freedom enables Tea Cake and Janie to reinvent their lives even as they grapple with and sometimes succumb to the pains of poverty and the complexity of human emotion. With Tea Cake in the Everglades, Janie enters a new community: "All night now the jooks clanged and clamored. Pianos living three lifetimes in one. Blues made and used right on the spot. Dancing, fighting, singing, crying, laughing, winning and losing love every hour. Work all day for money, fight all night for love" (125). The liveliness of the Everglades emerges from the continuous migration of Black workers "ugly from ignorance and broken from being poor" (ibid.). Despite the romantic portrayal of music, emotion, and struggle, the narrator does not obscure the presence of poverty and desperation that accompanies these Black migrants. Dangerous freedom, then, indicates multiple and often gendered expressions of those seeking life beyond the confines of established boundaries for behavior and community.

The isolation of Killicks's farm and the prosperity of Starks's store contrast greatly with the precarity of those working on the muck.

---

12. Toni Morrison first uses the term to describe the fictional character Cholly Breedlove in *The Bluest Eye*, 159–60.

13. See Rosalie Murphy Baum, "Alcoholism and Family Abuse in *Maggie* and *The Bluest Eye*," in *Toni Morrison's The Bluest Eye,* edited and with an introduction by Harold Bloom (New York: Bloom's Literary Criticism, 2007), 3–18; and Cyrus Pattell, *Negative Liberties: Morrison, Pynchon, and the Problem of Liberal Ideology* (Durham; London: Duke University Press, 2001).

Sadly, the efforts to combat that feeling of unpredictability come in the form of domestic violence. As the crowds return to the Everglades for the new season, Tea Cake resolves to assault Janie: "Being able to whip her reassured him in possession. . . . Everybody talked about it next day in the fields. It aroused a sort of envy in both men and women. The way he petted and pampered her as if those two or three face slaps had nearly killed her made the women see visions and the helpless way she hung on him made men dream dreams" (140). While it's clear that all of Janie's intimate relations result in misogynist violence and/or exploitation, the degree to which her subjection to abuse emerges from anxieties about her association with flight and mobility may be less apparent. "Tea Cake, you sho is a lucky man," the Black migrant Sop-de-Bottom expresses, indicating how Janie's violent subjugation provides a feeling of hope on his errant journey (ibid.). Although Tea Cake strikes Janie to keep her in place, his abuse provokes dreams of upward mobility for him and those Black migrants who witness his relationship to Janie. Just as Starks's blows against Janie affirmed his masculinist assertion of position in Eatonville, Tea Cake and the other Black migrants imagine moving into a place of power by stifling Janie's.

While critical interpretations[14] of the novel emphasize Janie's ability to develop and exercise her voice in the context of patriarchal authority, the confrontation between her intimate partners over competing visions of mobility problematize the very meaning of racial community itself. Janie and her masculine counterparts participate in the desire for migration and movement characteristic of their historical era, but their distinct versions of mobility suggest an incompatibility that troubles the basis upon which the formation of community as a possibility of progress is determined. The performance of conflict functions on at least three levels. First, the scene

---

14. See, for examples, Deborah E. McDowell, "New Directions for Black Feminist Criticism," *Black American Literature Forum* 14.4 (Winter 1980): 153–59; Calvin Hernton, "The Sexual Mountain and Black Women Writers," *Black American Literature Forum* 18.4 (Winter 1984): 139–45; Michael Awkward, *Inspiriting Influences: Tradition, Revision, and Afro-American Women's Novels* (New York: Columbia University Press, 1989); and Cheryl A. Wall, "Mules and Men and Women: Zora Neale Hurston's Strategies of Narration and Visions of Female Empowerment," *Black American Literature Forum* 23.4 (Winter 1989): 661–80.

of intimate antagonism is acted out in front of other characters. Second, the performance of conflict pushes the narrative forward, compelling Janie's flight from various romantic partners and communities. Third, the scene of intimate struggle forces a confrontation with competing visions of racial collectivity in the New Negro era. Accommodation, racial uplift, and dangerous freedom fail to establish a communal ethos capable of nurturing the intimate, intraracial bonds so central to the expansive view of mobility animating a period of Black migration.

Narratives of confinement and mobility pervade the writing of the Negro Renaissance era, especially in texts featuring Black female protagonists. Female Negro Renaissance protagonists reiterate the themes of sexual self-possession and intimate antagonisms as these heroines negotiate life under Jim Crow segregation and the process of turning segregation into congregation signified by the tension between confinement and escape. The explorations of the complexity of Black community formation during the New Negro era consistently return to this tension as these texts represent and reimagine Black mobility, community, and therefore Black spatiality.

Analyses of intimate antagonisms develop what Farrah Jasmine Griffin calls the "Black migration narrative" in relation to the movement away from racial terror, the adjustment to urban life, *and* the intraracial aesthetics of mobility itself. Hurston, and many other Black writers and artists, repeatedly depicts the dialectic between confinement and flight within the context of Black intraracial space. The formation of Black spatiality, in the process of developing and creating Negro art and expression, grapples with the conflicts that arise among a group forging a basis for and concept of collectivity. These intimate antagonisms produce an aesthetic form that also incorporates *intraracial* mobility as the basis for a new language of transformation, community, and space. "Internal migrations," in this sense, reference the portrayals of mobility that Black characters undertake in opposition to the sense of confinement imposed by narrow constructions of racial community. They take, as starting point, the process of imagining the obstacles to and possibilities for racial collectivity through the portrayal of intimate antagonism.

Nella Larsen's *Quicksand*[15] (1928), for example, already portrays frustration in the 1920s over the lost sense of political collectivity that should serve as the imagined foundation of knowledge and politics within the movement of Black people from the South to the North. There are pitfalls, the novel exhibits, in the emphasis on constant flight, just as there are in the constant pursuit of a preconceived home. *Quicksand* neither romanticizes southern Black life nor celebrates the urban Black aspiring class.

Helga Crane hates them all: "The South. Naxos. Negro education" (3). The beginning of *Quicksand* situates a brooding Helga Crane contemplating the thwarted wishes of middle-class southern Black life. Within the segregated South, Helga identifies another space of confinement. "This great community," she thinks, is "no longer a school. It had grown into a machine" (4). The school, in the administration's efforts to exemplify White "magnanimity" and to refute the ideology of Black inferiority, saps the community of its vitality: "Life had died out of it" (4). Trying to respond to and gain recognition from whiteness purges innovation and individualism, in her estimation. During a visit to the school, a southern White preacher complements and threatens the students about knowing their place. "There would be no race problem," he argues, "if all Negroes would only take a leaf out of the book of Naxos and conduct themselves in the manner of the Naxos products" (3). Reducing the students to "products" of the school machine and denying their humanity, he continues that Naxos Negroes "had good sense and they had good taste. They knew enough to stay in their places and that . . . showed good taste" (3). He wants to urge them to find contentment in their position. Despite the audience's appearance of polite respectability, his emphases on the puritan work ethic and religious passivity inspire resentment, expressed as intraracial cynicism and impatience.

Such ideologies about normativity, gender, race, and space emerge from and reflect the enclosures of the White spatial imaginary. George Lipsitz describes this racialized spatial ideology as

---

15. Nella Larsen, *Quicksand* (1928; New Brunswick: Rutgers University Press, 1986). Cited parenthetically throughout.

structuring feelings and social institutions that idealize "homogeneous spaces, controlled environments, and predictable patterns of design and behavior."[16] Lipsitz also describes a Black spatial imaginary that features a "socially shared understanding of the importance of public space as well as its power to create new opportunities and life chances."[17] If, as Ruth Wilson Gilmore argues, "a geographical imperative lies at the heart of every struggle for social justice,"[18] then the Black spatial imaginary insists that racial struggles for justice, or the Black radical tradition, necessitate "the creation of a counter social warrant with fundamentally different assumptions about place."[19]

If the school in Naxos indicates "racial uplift," Larsen's description illustrates a poignant critique of that school of thought and of the Black southerners who promote it. As Helga ponders, the problem does not lie with the students or with their ability to repeat the academic lessons offered at school. The problem is "the fault of the method, the general idea behind the system," whereby the material is "badly prepared for its purpose" (4). If the purpose is improvement or "uplift," confining Black young people to White expectations fails them again and again. Her reflections on the racial politics of Naxos compel Helga's desire to flee the South.

Hazel Carby argues that Black migration problematizes the role of Black intellectuals, especially their attempt to speak for or represent a "unitary people" and their hegemony over literary, political, and cultural practices as falling within the exclusive purview of the Black elite.[20] The diversification of the Black population and the services, organizations, and unions that respond to such a population's varied needs and experiences challenges the Talented Tenth's respectable, masculinist, and heteronormative leadership model for representing Black people and racial uplift. If the New Negro Move-

---

16. George Lipsitz, *How Racism Takes Place* (Philadelphia: Temple University Press, 2011), 29.

17. Ibid., 52.

18. Ruth Wilson Gilmore, "Fatal Couplings of Power and Difference," *Professional Geographer* 54.1 (2002): 16.

19. Lipsitz, *How Racism Takes Place*, 54.

20. Hazel Carby, *Reconstructing Womanhood: The Emergence of the Afro-American Woman Novelist* (New York; Oxford: Oxford University Press, 1987), 166.

ment was driven primarily by Black men demanding their legal rights as citizens, then Marcus Garvey, the washer women, Blues artists, and Black socialists provided an expanded view.

These creative texts form part of the cultural arm of that period's political struggle. The argument that liberal ideologies about the role of culture in justifying "normative social relations and the liberal nation-state"[21] is largely uncontested in analyses of Black literature from the 1920s and '30s. Key analytical readings of New Negro literature emphasize its claims to the dominant definition of humanity as the basis for recognition and inclusion.[22] Certainly, Negro Renaissance writers repeatedly articulated a belief in the role of expressive culture in challenging the ideology of Black inferiority. As poet, author, critic, and diplomat James Weldon Johnson argued, "The status of the Negro in the United States is more a question of national mental attitude toward the race than of actual conditions. And nothing will do more to change that mental attitude and raise his status than a demonstration of intellectual parity by the Negro through the production of literature and art."[23] Alain Locke's edited volume *The New Negro* (1925) celebrated Black intellectualism and unique aesthetic achievements while challenging the dominant exoticization and marginalization of Black cultural works and national presence. New Negro public and strident voices endeavored politically and culturally for the recognition of their legal rights as citizens and to fashion new images of Black people that would contest the disparaging caricatures of Black men and women as coons, bucks, mammies, and jezebels.

In the Black Belt of 1928, the year of *Quicksand*'s publication, tremendous poverty and the illiteracy and desperation that accompany racial segregation and oppression pervade Southern Black life. Caricatures of African Americans as lazy hide legally sanctioned discrimination and servile, degraded labor. The perception of Black people as ignorant masks Jim Crow segregation in education and

---

21. Roderick Ferguson, *Aberrations in Black: Toward a Queer of Color Critique* (Minneapolis: University of Minnesota Press, 2004), 25.
22. Gates, Huggins.
23. James Weldon Johnson, *The Book of American Negro Poetry* (New York: Harcourt Brace, 1922), 9.

the inferior state of Black schools. This is the culture of segregation. The "smoldering resentment" that Helga recognizes in the Naxos's student body engages the activists and agitators who established an invaluable intracommunal critique about the feelings of confinement and compulsion towards escape that pervade the literature of the New Negro era.

Like Hurston's protagonist Janie Crawford, Helga Crane also wants her past revealed, the history of sexual exploitation, betrayal, and abandonment that fuels her impatience with middle-class Black leaders' emphases on accommodation and gender normativity. Her migrations to Chicago, Harlem, and Denmark are not haphazard; they correspond with her struggle to reconnect with family and to "organize" her family life and history. By organize I mean her ability to represent, create coherence, and incorporate her ancestral past of exploitation into her narrative of Black resistance and Black communal life. Yet Helga is exoticized in Denmark, silenced in the South, and humiliated in the North. Each site presents her with a representation of "home" through relatives, racial community, and even marriage, but in refusing the complexity of her humanity reinforces the pattern of confinement from which she seeks to flee.

Rather than Black women knowing what to forget, as in Hurston's novel, the Black middle class in *Quicksand* tries to separate from that complex history, from a collective past left unexamined and unincorporated in the vision of uplift and resistance. In her romantic connection to James Vayle, her feelings of disquietude become intolerable. Helga's silence about her rebellious sentiments and unsavory past enable him to become "one of the community and so beyond the need or the desire to discuss its affairs and its failings with an outsider. She was, she knew, in a queer indefinite way a disturbing factor" (7). Helga's position as source of shame and source of pride in her coupling with James provokes a contradictory sensation of shame and power within her. Negro society, "she had learned, was as complicated and as rigid in its ramifications as the highest strata of white society. If you couldn't prove your ancestry and connections, you were tolerated, but you didn't 'belong'" (8). The opening of *Quicksand*, like *Their Eyes Were Watching God*, gives precedence to the complexity of intraracial relations and stages the conflict between the possibilities for community against the desire for escape.

Scenes of confinement and fantasies of flight find representation in the context of intraracial dynamics and relations and not exclusively at the color line in opposition to White supremacy. Grappling with these complex and contentious portrayals of Black life emphasizes intraracial relations as a valuable source for the development of New Negro Movement politics, especially the considerations of community in relation to leadership, class, and gender. The novel, like *Their Eyes Were Watching God*, is a moving narrative. Apart from depicting narratives of movement, such novels are *moving* in their attempt to make fluid the meaning of racial community. Affectively, they are *moving* through their portrayals of intimate desires and antagonisms that move readers into the position of witness. The movement away from confinement within the White spatial imaginary and towards a more expansive conception of racial politics and community also moves the Black female protagonist onto center stage in the drama that unfolds in the intimate quarters of Black life.

Quicksand features a Black female protagonist whose narrative focuses on the prohibition against representations of Black female desire. "Pleasure and danger," as Deborah McDowell describes in her important Introduction to Larsen's two novels, consider how the very act of representing Black female sexuality is rooted "in the artistic politics of the Harlem Renaissance."[24] Like Janie Crawford, Helga Crane embodies the desires, mobility, and spatial transgressions that provoke intraracial responses to the dialectic between confinement and flight that structure Negro Renaissance literature and the aesthetics of intraracial conflict that these texts reveal. Hurston and Larsen raise questions about notions like "respectability" and representation that have been central to Black literary studies. These terms emphasize the conflict over how Black people are seen and, secondarily, how they perceive each other. But Hurston and Larsen deny the hegemony of White conceptions of sexuality, behavior, pleasure,

---

24. Deborah E. McDowell, introduction to *Quicksand; and, Passing* (New Brunswick, NJ: Rutgers University Press, 1986), xiv.

aesthetics, and intimacy. Their representations show that they considered such concerns about sexuality, pleasure, and desire as central to Black identity, community, politics, aesthetics, and activism.

Despite anxieties about gendered and racial normativity, Black authors like Hurston, Larsen, and Wallace Thurman, as we shall see, examine life behind closed doors anyway. Their work indicates a certain disregard for the White gaze when it comes to representing Black intimate life and its relation to the development of Black radical politics.

YOUR BLACK AINT LIKE MINE: INTIMATE ANTAGONISMS AND GENDER POLITICS

*There was no place in the world for a girl
as black as she anyway*

—WALLACE THURMAN, *THE BLACKER THE BERRY*

Wallace Thurman's *The Blacker the Berry*[25] (1929) opens with two epigraphs that configure the dialectic between confinement and escape. "The blacker the berry / The sweeter the juice" is a Negro folk saying from which the novel takes its title. Connected to this statement is an excerpt from Countee Cullen: "My color shrouds me in."[26] These two excerpts situate the value of blackness against its perception as burden. In this way, these opening statements stage confinement and flight as structuring themes for the proceeding narrative. Skin color in these articulations represents another visible sign of Black oppression. Because fairer skin indicates a history of interracial sex and Black women's sexual exploitation, colorism constitutes a paradoxical basis for measuring one's degree of value within a White-dominated society haunted by the history of disavowing gendered and racist violence. Worked out in the intimate quarters that Black people occupy in a segregated society, colorism becomes a site for

---

25. Cited parenthetically throughout.
26. Countee Cullen, "The Shroud of Color," in *Countee Cullen: Collected Poems*, edited by Major Jackson (New York: Library of America, 2013).

intimate antagonisms over the terms of inclusion and recognition intraracially.

It is precisely this expansive view of mobility that shapes the many narratives of Black female protagonists on the move during the New Negro era. Black women in *Their Eyes Were Watching God* and other novels often occupy the roles of migrant, witness, and critic. Janie's friend Phoebe functions in the narrative as the audience for Janie's story. In other words, Janie's return is to a home she finds in her opportunity to narrate her experiences of romance, marriage, labor, disappointment, and desire. The roles of migrant, witness, and critic in fiction refract the lived realities of Black women during that era. Domestic and other forms of servile labor along with the policing of Black women's bodies and behavior indicate the association between Black female migrants and confinement. As Hazel Carby notes, the "migrating black woman could be variously situated as a threat to the progress of the race; a threat to the establishment of a respectable urban black middle class; a threat to congenial black and white middle-class relations; and a threat to the formation of black masculinity in an urban environment."[27] Black sociopolitical concerns about the spatial and sensual mobility of Black female bodies limit the spirit of migration that was not confined to physical geography. Even though "reality never matched the dream of the Great Migration,"[28] the building of extensive intraracial networks and the exercise of a new definition of agency through mobility and flight participated in shaping the meaning and possibilities of community.

Emma Lou, the female protagonist of Thurman's novel, represents a character for whom dark skin becomes the impetus for her successive migrations and her awakening to the radical possibility of Black identity. Colorism, the sociocultural privileging of fairer skin color, structures Emma Lou's interaction with Black people from the Midwest, to the West, and eventually to the Northeast. Emma Lou's movements compared to Helga's and Janie's recourse to mobility as a means reimagine the meaning of racial community. Nevertheless, Emma Lou's dark skin challenges the tragic mulatta narrative and

---

27. Carby, *Reconstructing Womanhood*, 153.
28. Ibid.

archetype in order to force a consideration of colorism intraracially as well as the impossible demand for homogeneity as the basis for recognition and intimacy. How are gender and color written into an ideology of form intraracially? At the beginning of the novel, Emma Lou has begun "to feel that her luscious black complexion was somewhat of a liability, and that her marked color variation from the other people in her environment was a decided curse. Not that she minded being black, being a Negro necessitated having a colored skin, but she did mind being too black" (9). Her feelings about blackness represent her internalization of a previous generation's emphasis on marrying well and lighter as the means to sustain position and secure future possibility. Although she experiences such demands as oppressive, Emma Lou quickly reanimates such affect as she migrates throughout the United States.

In the various locations from and to which Emma Lou flees, other Black people perceive her as proof of the stain and stigma of blackness. She is born in Boise, Idaho, to a family of "blue veins" who imagine themselves as so superior because of their fair skin that their "motto must be 'Whiter and whiter every generation,' until the grandchildren of the blue veins could easily go over into the white race and become assimilated so that problems of race would plague them no more" (19). Despite this imperative, Emma Lou's mother marries Jim Morgan, a man whose appearance marks him, perhaps, as coming "from one of the few families originally from Africa, who could not boast of having been seduced by some member of the southern aristocracy" (20). Emma Lou inherits her father's dark skin, and by contrast to the other blue veins reminds upwardly mobile Black people of the relationship between sexual reproduction and racial identity. The memory of the plantation and its sexual economy[29] connects mobility and desire in Emma Lou's narrative.

The University of Southern California is Emma Lou's choice for higher education. The promise of anonymity and busyness in an urban center give her the false belief that the modern city of Los

---

29. See Adrienne Davis, "'Don't Let Nobody Bother Yo' Principle': The Sexual Economy of American Slavery," in *Sister Circle: Black Women and Work,* edited by Sharon Harley and the Black Women and Work Collective (New Brunswick, NJ: Rutgers University Press, 2002), 103–27.

Angeles will distract Black people from their ideas about skin color, value, and community. Sadly, she finds that the people with whom she would like to socialize share the same attitudes of the blue veins from Idaho. At USC she also finds herself outside of the Black social sets composed of children from well-to-do Southern families, for they also migrated West "to live where they would have greater freedom and greater opportunity for both their children and themselves" (58). This wish, however, accompanies the desire to "keep their children and grandchildren from having dark complexions" (ibid.). If community connection and upward mobility signify the maintenance of fair skin, Emma Lou has little chance to be perceived as socially or sexually desirable among other Black people in California.

Emma Lou, however, also rejects the constraints on her body and mobility that her Black classmates create. Instead, she allows Weldon Taylor to lead her "off the little path they had been following" while she visits home during the summer break (62). This detour with Taylor brings her willingly to her first intimate sexual contact (63). Images of mobility surround her sexual experience with Taylor. Submitting to him and the "momentary physical pain" of her first encounter with sex transports her "into a new and incomparably satisfying paradise" (ibid.). The experience also moves her away from her mother's and grandmother's "Blue Vein" warnings about choosing a suitable mate and class mobility, a decision that foreshadows Emma Lou's ongoing geographical and ideological movement from the confinement of color prejudice. Even still, Taylor, without warning, decides to become a Pullman porter, a decision he makes due to the servile labor that confines him as a hotel waiter and his desire to earn money to increase his options for mobility (68). Their intimate relationship develops the theme of confinement versus flight in the novel as Emma Lou struggles to unlearn the intraracial antagonisms that characterize her experiences.

In Harlem Emma Lou again encounters segregation and the absence of privacy. From the real estate agents who profit from racism in producing "Negro Harlem" to the landlady who suspiciously asks "Ain't you got a job yet?," Emma Lou repeatedly learns that for a dark-skinned Black girl, life presents many obstacles (94, 103). Emma Lou's movements do not allow the conception of Black community to be bounded by geographical space. From Boise, to USC, to Harlem, her pursuit of Black community as a symbol of her acceptance and belonging is thwarted at each stop: "There was no place for her in the world. She was too black, black is a portent of evil, black is a sign of bad luck" (254). Like Janie Crawford, Emma Lou recognizes through her geographical flights that the intimate antagonisms over color and gender transcend region and do not solve the problems of her past. Mobility in the novel and the circulation of blackness still animates the themes of Black spatial and intimate relations. Although the novel does not resolve these tensions, it does illustrate how intraracial relations become a key site of struggle over the meaning of racial community.

The staging of intimate antagonisms in the literature of the New Negro era forces a reckoning with the importance of unity, the need to examine the problematic relationship between scholar and community, the significance of broadening conceptions of social transformation, and the central role of intraracial relations in transformative politics. Although these texts do not always resolve the tensions they portray, when there are breakthroughs they often come through depictions of intimate, intraracial antagonisms. Also, these ruptures depend on the symbolic depiction of the Black female subject. The exercise of erotic agency, professional mobility, and even community advocacy, as we have seen, portray Black female protagonists challenging the conventions of confinement in plot and, metacritically, in politics. These challenges, however, also shoulder them symbolically with the burdens of representing intimate antagonisms. Because the depiction of intimate, intraracial antagonisms begin during the periods of the Great Black Migration and the New Negro Eras, representations of the Black woman are central to engaging how these conflicts.

•

New Negro Movement activists placed an enervating amount of stress on Black cultural expression as key to the move for recognition from dominant White culture. Indeed, what many scholars through the ages have critiqued most about the period is the presumed pandering to liberal White sensibilities, both in terms of the pathway to publication and the terms for recognition. These critiques and evaluations of the era center the "color line" in their assessments, cognizant of the economic, political, and cultural power that the dominant White culture wielded (and continues to wield) in the realm of power traditionally conceived. Key concepts emerging from the era like "respectability," "the burden of representation," and even the meaning of "Black letters and culture" owe their origin to the conscious fabrication of Black literature and identity that took precedence during this period.

Undeniably, Black artists, thinkers, and personalities understood the impact of anti-Black racism on their efforts. Despite one's position in the Black intellectual elite, one's parentage in established Northern Black families, routes from the West Indies, or self-proclaimed narrative of "bootstrap" pulling, the realities of anti-Black racism crosscut the experiences and identities of Black people collectively. The contradictions of Jim Crow segregation notwithstanding, the system and culture of racism depended upon political, cultural, economic, psychological, and spatial arrangements that granted Whites unfair advantages in both policy and practice.

New Negro activists, aware of the multifaceted dimensions of anti-Black racism, highlighted Black letters as *one* strategic tactic for accessing the benefits of recognition and inclusion as equal citizens in the U.S. polity. While many scholars[30] of the New Negro era have rightly acknowledged Black people's emphasis on humanism to the struggle for equality, too many of their analyses marginalize or overlook the centrality of intraracial conflicts over the definition of "humanism" and over intraracial debates about the bases for recognition and inclusion. Foremost among these over-

---

30. See, for example, W. E. B. Du Bois, "Criteria of Negro Art," *The Crisis* 32 (1926): 290; George S. Schuyler, "The Negro Art Hokum," *The Nation* 122 (1926): 662–63; Carl Van Vechten, "The Negro in Art: How Shall He Be Portrayed, A Symposium," *The Crisis* 31 (1926): 219; Huggins, *Harlem Renaissance*; David Levering Lewis, *When Harlem Was in Vogue* (New York: Oxford University Press, 1979); Gilbert Osofsky, "Symbols of the Jazz Age: The Negro and Harlem Discovered," *American Quarterly* 17.2 (Summer 1965): 229–38; Gerald Early, "The Quest for a Black Humanism," *Daedalus* 135.2 (Spring 2006): 91–104; and Skip G. Gates, "Of Negroes Old and New," *Transition* 46 (1974): 44–50, 52–58.

sights is Black people's own concerns about the terms upon which they define themselves as a community united against a racism more complex and with more complicated consequences than have been acknowledged.

As Raymond Williams[31] writes, traces of the lived experiences of a community, distinct from the institutional and ideological organization of the society, can be found in the work of poets and novelists. His description of the "structure of feeling" pervades intraracial representations of conflict in Black American literature. Such a view coincides with the Black radical tradition. The foci on White recognition and related hopes for political and social transformation reduce African descendants to people without histories or cultures. Instead, the Black radical tradition proposes a different conception of "being" and therefore of revolution.

The alternative modes and systems of being "preserved" in culture champion Black literary expression as a valuable site for Black radical politics. The dialectic between confinement and escape thus asserts humanity, as well as its redefinition, from the vantage point of intraracial tensions and possibilities. The intraracial thus becomes a site and fomenting ground, our authors indicate, for the considerations of staging resistance. For them, resistance begins not necessarily at the confrontation with whiteness but with the exploration of intraracial explorations of ships and trees, and of confinement and flight. With their emergence in the period of Great Black Migration, Black writers take intimate antagonisms into the realm of public struggles for liberation.

---

31. Raymond Williams, *Marxism and Literature* (Oxford: Oxford University Press, 1977).

CHAPTER 2

Intimate Antagonisms and Double Consciousness in the Debate over Integration

> *Accompanying and indeed constituting the subjective aspect of the change in the social structure was the attitude of the Negro himself.*
>
> —ST. CLAIR DRAKE AND HORACE R. CAYTON, *BLACK METROPOLIS: A STUDY OF NEGRO LIFE IN A NORTHERN CITY*

ACCORDING TO St. Clair Drake and Horace R. Cayton, Black people's perspectives determine the significance of the political and social transformations taking place in the post–New Negro Era. Integration emerges as a key concept in the debate over the so-called Negro problem in U.S. political and social life as calls for unity and democracy occupy the discursive space of the interwar and postwar periods.[1] Intraracial dialogues and debates over race, space, and community don't disappear after the New Negro Renaissance era,

---

1. See Nikil Pal Singh, *Black Is a Country: Race and the Unfinished Struggle for Democracy* (Cambridge, MA: Harvard University Press, 2004); Carole Anderson, *Eyes Off the Prize: The United Nations and the African American Struggle for Human Rights, 1944–1955* (Cambridge; New York: Cambridge University Press, 2003); George Lipsitz, *American Studies in a Moment of Danger* (Minneapolis: University of Minnesota Press, 2001); Mary Helen Washington, *The Other Blacklist: The African American Literary and Cultural Left of the 1950s* (New York: Columbia University Press, 2014); and William J. Maxwell, *F. B. Eyes: How J. Edgar Hoover's Ghostreaders Framed African American Literature* (Princeton: Princeton University Press, 2015) on this period of racial representation, the Cold War, and U.S. domestic and foreign politics. The symbolic position of Black Americans in the U.S. polity becomes a source of critique or an opportunity for fabricating a progressive racial history.

but they do escalate into differing points of view as the struggles against racism and poverty continue to build momentum. The internationalism and local engagements of Black affiliates of the Communist Party USA, antilynching campaigns of the National Association for the Advancement of Colored Peoples, Ida B. Wells journalistic activism against lynching and for the full enfranchisement of all U.S. citizens regardless of race or gender, the mobilization and organization of Black military personnel, the ongoing Black Clubwomen's movement, and continuing Black migration into urban locations nurture the vital intraracial town-hall forums that foster the formation of the civil rights movement and debates about Black subjectivity despite increasing calls for integration in an increasingly hostile racial climate.

Intimate, intraracial antagonisms figure prominently in Cayton and Drake's groundbreaking study *Black Metropolis: A Study of Negro Life in a Northern City*[2] (1945). As the authors demonstrate, in intraracial conversations Black people "take out in talk" discontent with the slow progress of their economic, labor, and political advancement. This talk, however, doesn't end with Black peoples' frustration and condemnation of White America but extends to the critique of Race, men and women, the Black middle class, and the perceived lack of Black solidarity: "I can't say that I don't like a jig, because I'm one myself. But they sure won't help one another"; "Dagoes will help one another; Japs'll help one another—everything but a nigger"; "You know, I've seen colored people in many countries, but ain't none of them like the American Negro. He won't co-operate for nothing!" (724).

Cayton and Drake's attention to intraracial relations and conflicts challenge the standard approach to the so-called Negro problem by centering Black people's complex lives and experiences in the context of racial subordination, their conflicts and frustrations with the direction and pace of social change, and their willingness to wage critiques inter- *and* intraracially as necessary to the redefinition of progress and integration. In place of a seamless history of racial integration and progress, Black writers and thinkers in the post–New

---

2. Cited parenthetically throughout.

Negro era do not leave a record of agreement on the topic of integration but instead question and therefore broaden the potential meaning of integration and radical politics. The relationship between Black subjects and themselves, as well as the relationship between the Black subject and the community, emerge as central questions. Post–New Negro literature offers foundational and often overlooked insight into the meaning of integration in the march towards civil rights mobilizations. The literary depictions of intimate antagonisms do not posit freedom dreams as being fulfilled by White recognition and offers of integration. Centering the meditations on Black subjectivity in an era of state-based lip service to hollow notions of integration, these writers instead exhibit concern for the complexity of Black lives in the context of public debates about integration.

Intimate antagonisms in 1940s and '50s Black U.S. literature challenge notions of social, national, and economic integration in favor of an increasingly radical representation of Black humanity, subjectivity, and community. Depictions of Black consciousness and fractured intimacies shift from a prioritization of spatial relations to first-person narratives that bring attention to Black psychic and interior life. With an investment in radical ways of knowing, Black writers, scholars, and activists question the very definition and role of integration to the Black radical tradition. Although visions of a unified community may underlie these representations, Black literature of this period rarely offers its readers the fulfillment of such righteous desires. Abuse, addiction, and abandonment more often fuel post–New Negro Renaissance literature. Reckoning with the creative portrayal of conflict in the midst of ongoing activism against the racial state, we find ourselves confronting the painful and exciting possibility of imagining how intraracial conceptions of integration could reshape the nation and the dreams of Black liberation.

If Black people's attitudes constitute and accompany the changes in social structure, how do we account for the sentiment of intraracial strife that the sociologists note? Cayton and Drake's *Black Metropolis,* in their discussion of Bronzevilles in the United States and in their anecdotes about intraracial criticism in the postwar period, refracts literary concerns of the same era. Black literature from the post–New Negro era to the beginning of the civil rights movement intensifies its portrayals of intimate, intraracial antagonisms. During this time readers confront the first depictions of intraracial rape, abuse, and even murder in Richard Wright's *Native Son* (1940) and Ann Petry's "Like a Winding Sheet" (1945), for example. Representations of familial fragmentation (*Maud Martha, Go Tell It on the Mountain,* and *Raisin in the Sun*) and individual isolation ("Sonny's Blues," *Invisible Man,* and *Black Boy*) heighten the literature's emphasis on the crises confronting the meaning of integration for the Black community and the Black subject.

DOUBLY CONSCIOUS?: INTIMATE ANTAGONISMS AND INTRARACIAL CONSCIOUSNESS

Chester Himes's 1945 novel *If He Hollers Let Him Go*[3] is the first-person narrative of a few days in the life of Robert Jones. Readers closely follow Bob's unspoken ruminations, tormented dreams, and social interactions as he grapples with the impending sense of doom that he believes pursues him because he is a Black man in the United States. The novel in structure and theme exemplifies the emphases on Black interior life and intimate antagonisms during the period. Although Bob negotiates the threats of lynching, the draft, and self-destruction, the novel pivots around his relationship to and desire for Alice. Their potential intimate relationship is paradoxically a source of both possibility and self-abnegation in the fully racialized context of California and the nation itself. In Himes's novel, the depictions of intimate antagonism and Black subjectivity combine in a powerful critique of integration.

"'I'll admit I don't want to go into the Army.' I said. 'But that's not the reason I want to keep my job.' I paused, then told him, 'I want to get married,'" Bob Johnson grudgingly admits to the White shipyard boss Mac (173). It's not so much that Bob is half-hearted about his desire to marry Alice, the fair-skinned, wealthy social worker with whom he's making future plans. Committing to Alice and marriage,

---

3. Chester Himes, *If He Hollers Let Him Go* (New York: Thunder's Mouth, 1945). Cited parenthetically throughout.

Bob loses doubt: "I could take anything the white folks wanted to put on me, as long as I had this. Because this was it; I knew this was it" (170), he relishes, after kissing Alice's lips. The problem, however, is that the possibility of wedded bliss that Alice offers demands that he acquiesce to segregation, apologize to his White racist co-workers, and keep his job building a naval destroyer.

As Bob conveys why he left Cleveland for Los Angeles, he describes West Coast racial dynamics: "It wasn't being refused employment in the plants so much. When I got here practically the only job a Negro could get was service in the white folks' kitchens. But it wasn't that so much. It was the look on the people's faces when you asked them about a job. Most of 'em didn't say right out they wouldn't hire me. They just looked so goddamned startled that I'd even asked. As if some friendly dog had come in through the door and said, 'I can talk'" (3). The silent refusals coupled with the presumption of Black inferiority seek to rob him of his humanity. Comparing himself to a friendly but speaking dog, Bob experiences racial discrimination as a reminder of the limit of Black inclusion. Maintaining a position of servility to White people and submission to segregation's protocols continue to define integration as an acceptance of self-abnegation. When Bob witnesses the processes of Japanese internment, or "Little Riki Oyana singing 'God Bless America' and going to Santa Anita with his parents next day," he begins to feel his fear (3).

Managing national concerns about security and citizenship produces race as central to domestic and international visions about the place of the United States in the world. The interwar and Cold War periods bear witness to an important shift in the nation's attitude towards and discourses about African Americans and other racially subordinated groups. By the end of World War II, White supremacy becomes an undeniable "'Achilles heel' of U.S. foreign relations," whereby America's designs and policies of global expansion clash with ongoing and expanding racial strife domestically.[4] Accelerated modes for structuring racism through ghettoization, residential segregation, labor discrimination, welfare exclusion, police brutality,

---

4. Singh, *Black Is a Country*, 7.

and lynching challenged the ability of the United States to recruit the vast public into conformity with the hegemonic discourses of global *and* domestic security.[5] Even efforts to repackage Japanese Americans from enemies of the state into "model minorities" depended on sustaining the ideology of Black people as the forever inferior and subordinated minority group.[6] If Jim Crowism extended to African Americans' inclusion into the nation through exclusion and subordination, U.S. Cold War strategies meant proffering Black people's *integration* as a form of self-abnegation.

With the first bomb that falls on Pearl Harbor, a flood of racial animosity pervades the streets of Los Angeles. "Every time I stepped outside I saw a challenge I had to accept or ignore," Bob recalls, "I was the same colour as the Japanese and I couldn't tell the difference" (4). The feeling of being constantly prepared to fight or flee weighs heavily on Bob, so much so that he loses "twenty pounds in two weeks and my hands got to trembling" (4). The opening chapters of *If He Hollers* present us with a narrator suffering under the imposition of racial discrimination and terror. Given his options to accept or ignore the terms that would grant him a place in society, the remainder of the novel unfolds as a negotiation of those options. Integration and marginalization are not terms that Bob examines in relationship to anti-Black racism exclusively. When Bob witnesses a coterie of middle-class Black women, he sarcastically recounts their discussion. "We were just discussing the problems that confront the social worker in Little Tokyo . . . I was saying that first of all there must be some organization within the community through which a programme of integration may be instituted into the broader pattern of the community," one of the members summarizes (83). Responding, another chimes in, "And you know how they'll do even if they build a development down there; they'll allocate about one-fourth to Negroes and the rest to whites and Mexicans." Another adds, "What they should really do is stop all these Southern Negroes from coming into the city." The first speaker returns, offering that "the ghetto's

---

5. Ibid., 8.
6. Robert G. Lee, *Orientals: Asian Americans in Popular Culture* (Philadelphia: Temple University Press, 1999).

already formed. The problem now is how best to integrate the people of this ghetto into the life of the community" (84).

The discussion of integration the women's group elaborates is also representative of the dynamic between Bob and Alice. The two come from different class backgrounds, but more importantly they have distinct views on integration. For Alice, the path to happiness is through a patient acceptance of the racial status quo, in learning how to go along to get along in the segregated realities of the United States. Hard work and respectability inform how she performs in society as a way to advance economically and potentially gain White favor. She is employed as a social worker and therefore is positioned to work for the improvement of working-class lives. As the daughter of a successful doctor, she comes from a position of class privilege. These markers of behavior and privilege seem to present the long-standing conflict between working-class and aspiring-class Black people. Alice articulates the discourse of racial uplift and encourages Bob to align with such a program.

"One ever feels his two-ness," W. E. B. Du Bois writes: "an American, a Negro; two souls, two thoughts, two unreconciled strivings; two warring ideals in one dark body, whose dogged strength alone keeps it from being torn asunder."[7] For him, the history of Black Americans, and thus of Black subjectivity, "is the history of this strife," which Du Bois describes as a longing "to merge his double self into a better and truer self."[8] "Integration" within Black subjectivity emerges as a necessary foundation from which to ascend into the mode of spiritual transcendence that *The Souls of Black Folk* envisions. Integration therefore becomes conceivable not at the color line first, but within Black life, experience, and subjectivity.

The Souls of Black Folk was published in 1903, but the chapter "Of Our Spiritual Strivings" was previously featured in the literary journal *Atlantic* in 1897.[9] Despite critics' understanding of the sig-

---

7. W. E. B. Du Bois, *The Souls of Black Folk* (1903), edited by Henry Louis Gates Jr. and Terri Hume Oliver (New York: Bantam Books, 1989), 11.

8. Ibid.

9. See Dickson D. Bruce Jr., "W. E. B. Du Bois and the Idea of Double Consciousness," *American Literature: A Journal of Literary History, Criticism, and Bibliography* 64.2 (June 1992): 299–309.

nificance of the double-consciousness concept to the reading public at the turn of the century, Black writers during the Negro Renaissance era do not fully feature the idea as a primary literary figure. From the 1930s to the 1950s, Black writers begin to explore questions surrounding Black subjectivity and Black intimacy in relation to the debates about racial integration. In other words, during a period of increasing Black mobilizations against oppression, Black writers begin to use double consciousness to address intraracial subjectivities. Though we are all "split subjects," this is generally not portrayed, but always enacted. Through the literary depiction of intimate antagonisms, we witness the process of disintegration that challenges the dominant discourse of integration and posits alternative perspectives on liberation.

The terms of assimilation were an impossible game, since White subjectivity is built on dissociation from blackness. So, assimilation meant giving up Black subjectivity, a price few could actually pay. Yet, for the sake of the material and resource advantages, some tried to do so, by adjusting either their attitude or their style, or by other means. The question of integrating the duality of the Black subject had to grapple with what giving up the Black self would mean, and whether that price would actually lead to liberation. As it turns out, the dual selves Du Bois writes about usually lead to seeing that Eurocentric ontologies are empty, vapid, and alienating. So, one had the choice of being subordinated by racism but having subject integrity, or assimilating for advantages but having an empty shell of a self. These negotiations never stop.

Alice, for example, is unable to fully conform to the expectations of normativity that she espouses. Stella, one of the members of Alice's coterie, sees Alice's failed reproduction of normativity:

> [Stella] stepped past me and put her arm about Alice's waist and they went into the kitchen. I looked at Dimples and said, "Wanna dance?" [. . .]
>
> "Not with you," she said in a harsh, sullen voice, looking sidewise into the darkened kitchen.
>
> [. . .]

Alice and Stella were sitting side by side on the davenport, whispering. Dimples sat on the arm of the davenport watching them, her face a mask of sullen envy. (67)

Recognizing that Alice and Stella were engaged in an erotic encounter, Bob reacts violently: "I knew what was going on and I wasn't having any of it. I felt shocked, sickened. I went back into the room and said to Alice, 'You can't do this to me'" (67). Nonetheless, he internalizes the presumed pathology of Alice's sexual behavior: "I felt an odd sort of embarrassment for her; a sort of mixture of shame and betrayal and repulsion. I hoped I wouldn't have to see her for some time [. . .]. The night kept coming back in brown, dirty memories. Parts of my dream were mingled with them. I began feeling remorseful. I despised myself" (70).

"Every time I kiss you now I'm scared you might be laughing," Bob admits to Alice (93). Bob likens the presumed betrayal of Alice's erotic same-sex encounters to the possibility of her pursuing a White man sexually. Regarding Tom Leighton, Alice's White co-worker and political interlocutor, Bob muses, "She might be having an affair with Leighton sure enough, I thought. She wouldn't count that, just like she wouldn't count that stuff at Stella's. She'd probably be proud of it, I thought; probably feel that I shouldn't resent it even if I found out" (87).

Sexual competition fuels the protagonist's narrative of isolation, fear, and longing. Bob's critique of integration and uplift discourse emerges in his reading of Black aspirations for economic mobility: "Although Negro people such as Alice and her class had got enough bread—they prospered from it. No matter what had happened to them inside, they hadn't allowed it to destroy them outwardly; they had overcome their colour the only way possible in America—as Alice had put it, by adjusting themselves to the limitations of their race. They hadn't stopped trying, I gave them that much; they'd kept on trying, always would; but they had recognized their limit—a nigger limit" (150).

Sexual desire and sexual intimacy are key sites of conflict throughout the novel and thus the main vehicles for moving the narrative itself. Bob's role as focalizer as well as the attention to his inner life form a narrative contestation of the sexual iconography of the so-called Black brute. Without doubt, Bob repeatedly grasps at the most traditional features of patriarchal masculinity. Bob's consciousness therefore records and complicates his descent into violence as he negotiates the injuries of racist oppression through his intimate relations with Alice and himself.

If He Hollers Let Him Go, like other novels of the post–New Negro Renaissance era, raises the issue of intimate relations and antagonisms as central to grappling with the processes of elaborating social ideology and determining superstructure. The racial, and gendered, state's attempts to define and control the meaning and function of race, citizenship, and nation appear in Himes's representation of the culture of segregation, the war, and the shipyard. From an intraracial vantage point, however, the novel also compels readers to consider the culture, institutions, roles, and rituals that emerge from the ideologies of Black resistance struggles.

Himes's novels address the Black subject's isolation in relationship to the possibility for intraracial intimacy in the context of racial capitalism. In Bob's work on the superstructure of a military ship, the very question of integration begins with the obstacles confronting Black subjectivity and Black communal formations despite the dominant though hollow discourses of interracial integration and tolerance. The novel's reference to the ship's superstructure is also an allusion to Marxist theory. The ship, like society, echoes racial, gendered, and social relations. Government, military, and capitalism are organized by White patriarchal power. The lower sections of the ship are occupied by Black male workers. Black and White women labor in supporting positions though their physical and symbolic labor. Despite the racially promiscuous work environment, protecting White women is a proof of manhood that reinforces the culture of segregation. All workers, nonetheless, toil in support of the overall stability of the superstructure in the fight against fascism abroad while fostering racial and gendered divisions at home. Herbie Frieberger, the Jewish American labor organizer at the shipyard, downplays race in favor of the presumed universality of the class struggle, but the divisions between employers (leadermen) and welders, between the genders, and between the races reflect the culture of segregation and the sexual dynamics that reinforce it. The workers' material conditions (Madge's dive apartment in a rough, White working-class hotel; Bob's makeshift room in the apartment he shares with Ella Mae, her husband, and daughter) inform the superstructure that the workers labor to produce.

At the novel's conclusion, Bob escapes imprisonment for the attack on his White female co-worker but is nonetheless "sentenced" to serve in the army. Both represent forms of punishment: the refusal of his dream of marriage, and the prolongation of the threat of death and violence that he awakens to in the novel's first chapter.

The threat of death that pursues Bob throughout the novel can be seen as illustrating Hegel's lord/bondsman or master/slave dialectic. Relations of dominance structure how Hegel and others have theorized self-consciousness and the formation of subjectivity. Critiquing Hegel's model, Abdul JanMohamed departs from the strict and exclusive relationship between the master and slave in his theorization of the death-bound subject.[10] Examining Richard Wright's creative work, JanMohamed considers the novelist's repeated depictions of Black male characters being forced to witness a lynching in the narrative of their development into manhood. Black male subjectivity is thus formed, in large part, through the pervasive threat of death. For JanMohamed, this threat is also a mode of coercion, a force of both control and compulsion. The death-bound subject is compelled to conform to racial structures of domination. Black literature and culture, according to JanMohamed, are repositories for the depictions of and wisdom gained through the meditation on "the effectivity of the threat of death as a mode of coercion" (3). Such wisdom combines practical and theoretical knowledges about "the means and effort required to resist and, indeed, triumph over such coercion" that offers careful readers an "understanding of the psychological, social, political, and economic dynamics of the processes of oppression and resistance" (4).

---

10. Abdul JanMohamed, *The Death-Bound Subject: Richard Wright's Archaeology of Death* (Durham: Duke University Press, 2005). Cited parenthetically throughout.

Maintaining the emphasis on violence and domination, JanMohamed's important analysis utilizes Black cultural production to think about the Black radical tradition and makes room for the consideration of Black intersubjectivity. The development of Black intersubjectivity must contend with the perennial threat of death: "it is precisely by threatening to 'actualize' his potential or postponed death that the slave can rearticulate the death contract that binds him" (17). If holding on to life, under the terms of the death contract, requires the slave to accept his position as slave, then embracing death reveals and refuses the very terms of that binding contract. Life, in this context, looks like assimilating to the racial status quo, accepting blackness as abjection, and conforming to the persistent threat of death. In the willingness to risk death, however, the slave then "negates his social-death or his enslavement," and constitutes "his rebirth in a different subject-position" (17).

In his engagement with Wright's texts, JanMohamed sees the author as producing himself as a "suturing medium" occupying "a space between the world and these black subjects" and thereby becoming an "active, articulate 'witness for their living'" (32). Through literature Wright encounters the eyes and lives of those lynched Black bodies. In the struggle between life and death, "Wright not just occupies but embodies" the space of the Black male other who is also himself (34). Wright "survives this struggle by developing a compromise formation, a tactic that allows death to permeate his subjectivity while he keeps himself alive by shifting the center of his intellectual, emotional, and existential gravity to the stance of the observer: he stays alive by becoming a witness of the very process that is designed to form him as a socially dead being" (35–36). African American literature, in its meditation on the political, social, economic, and psychological effects of death as coercion and control, depicts Black intersubjectivity as a way to rethink Black subject formation, to signify the importance of intraracial intimacy, and to produce Black witnesses to both the pain and possibilities of imagining life anew. "As opposed to idiosyncratically individual subjects," these depictions portray collective characters that highlight the subject-position these figures have in common with regard to the experience of racist terror and oppression (33). Black intersubjectivity, therefore, is not secondary to color-line antagonisms but a challenge to the logic of recognition itself.

The emphasis on lynching in JanMohamed's theorization of the death-bound subject prioritizes anti-Black masculinity and relations between men over the possibility of examining a broader set of intraracial dynamics that include attention to gender and sexuality. He describes the subjection to death as emasculation (21). Although he importantly examines Black intersubjectivity, his analysis depends on gender-sameness, moving the struggle to the death between White and Black men to the struggle and possibility over death between Black men alone. Such a perspective ignores our understanding of what Frances Beal describes as "double jeopardy."[11] She critiques definitions of manhood and womanhood that align with the interests of U.S. capitalism:

> Many black women tended to accept the capitalist evaluation of manhood and womanhood and believed, in fact, that black men were shiftless and lazy, otherwise they would get a job and support their families as they ought to. Personal relationships between black men and women were thus torn asunder and one result has been the separation of man from wife, mother from child, etc.[12]

Women and especially Black women are relegated to the position of surplus labor supply, and yet bedroom politics (including sterilization as well as intimate antagonisms) reduce their role in the people's revolution. The exclusive emphasis on patriarchal structures over power renders their labor and laboring bodies as the "unthought" of Black consciousness and revolutionary subjectivity.

If, as JanMohamed argues, Black intersubjectivity reverses the death-bound subject, then intersectionality further erodes the supposed unitary master and what he must already repress for his assumed dominance. Everyday relations, in addition to lynching, reinforce the structure of the lord's dominance. His refusal of wom-

---

11. See Frances Beal, "Double Jeopardy: To Be Black and Female," in *The Black Woman: An Anthology*, edited by Toni Cade Bambara (New York: Washington Square Press, 1970), 109–22.

12. Ibid., 110.

en's labor as well as her social and psychological relations negates his singular power and disavows his dependency not only on the bondsman but also on the female in the Hegelian framework. Likewise, the revision of Hegel's master/slave in the conceptualization of the death-bound subject must also be expanded to account for other axes of power and frameworks of recognition.

Thus, neither Bob nor Lee Gordon in Himes's *Lonely Crusade* (1947)[13] can successfully stage their Leftist campaigns and struggles with death separate from intimate, intraracial antagonisms. As we saw in *If He Hollers,* intimate struggles consistently shape the protagonist's conception of himself in relation to his opposition to racism. *Lonely Crusade* portrays Lee Gordon, an African American college graduate who accepts a job as the first Black union organizer in Los Angeles during the World War II era. Quickly, the protagonist finds that he can trust no one, not the union officials, Black Communist organizers, the plant owner, or even his own wife. Gordon's lonely crusade to struggle and suffer for the idealism of freedom, justice, and equality make him confront the violent forces of racism as well as his own internalization of Black inferiority as he endeavors to unite Black and White workers. He recognizes that the monolithic label "the Negro" does little to aid him in his work: "How many times had he, Lee Gordon, used the term 'The Negro' with that pompous positiveness of ignorance to describe the individual emotions and reactions, appearances and mentalities, the character and souls of fifteen million people" (62). In his attempt to connect with "the Negro," he misses them completely. He admits that most Black Americans were strangers to him and "seemed as atypical to him as they appeared to whites" (ibid.). Gordon had "never visualized them in the farthest reaches of his imagination" and he had "never known where they lived or how they lived, but that they lived at all" (ibid.). Initially, it is his education and position as outside organizer that compel his sense that he is a stranger to working-class Black people. He desires to convince them of the opportunities that union membership offers to them but is instead met with their refusal to believe that any union would address the unique situation of Black people's

---

13. Cited parenthetically throughout.

lives. Rather than confront these arguments, Gordon is unable to establish mutual recognition with the very people he imagines himself working for. Instead, he concludes that oppression "had completely destroyed the moral fiber of an entire people" and that "the Negroes of America had actually become an inferior people" (70).

The ideology of Black inferiority blocks Gordon's efforts, as an educated, professional union organizer, to create a bond of recognition with other Black people that would allow him to be witness to their pain and produce the possibilities for new life. In his projection of inferiority onto the masses of working Black people and therefore his inability to work, Gordon finds himself "entangled in his own confusion, chagrined by his inability to make [a White union organizer] understand what he did not quite understand himself" (142). And in his urgency to be understood, and thus to understand himself, his thoughts constantly return to his wife, Ruth, and their intimate antagonism. "That was hopeless, *he told himself*. She could not even understand his necessity for dominance, or anything at all about his ego—his warped ego, his sickly dwarfed, cowardly, cringing ego that his fear had given to him. An ego that made a man beat his wife just to prove that he was stronger" (143). Again, the literary portrayal of the struggle for recognition in the process towards self-consciousness plays out in intimate antagonisms. When Ruth questions his decision to accept a higher paid position in the factory she asks him, "at the expense of me, Lee? Is that how you have to be true to yourself, by having us live in poverty and fear all of our lives?" (185). Ruth also works. Her employment is a constant source of conflict between the couple, as her job symbolizes for them his inability to assume a traditional role as breadwinner and therefore as a man. Ruth does not "understand the quality within him that had made him refuse the job—a quality that once she had been so proud of him for having—now she felt excluded by it and resentful of it" (ibid.). Neither Ruth nor Lee manages to share these deeper reflections with each other and in turn persist in battling each other over the understanding and recognition that would enable them to confront their racial realities together.

Once Lee Gordon gives in to his fantasies for Jackie, a White Communist charged with the task of seducing him to give the

Party sway over the union, he becomes "not a man, but once more a Negro" in Ruth's eyes (301). For Lee, the torment of recognizing the chasm between himself and Jackie and his wife's witnessing of his affair brings his thoughts again to Ruth: "But that he could have felt such a pity for a white woman as to destroy the love of his Negro wife would take no form but lunacy in his present state of mind" (306). The exposure of his relationship with Jackie and the demise of his marriage to Ruth inaugurate the rapid movement towards the novel's conclusion. Gordon's intimate conflicts and public struggles collide as the rumors of his affair with a White Communist woman damage his credibility with the union and with other Black workers. Although the novel ends with Ruth witnessing Gordon taking up the union banner from a fallen fellow organizer, the narrative insists that the Black man's crusade is much more informed by the possibilities of Black intersubjectivity than it is by loneliness.

Such Black literary portrayals and critiques of masculinity and Leftist organizing must address the presence and productions of Richard Wright. Wright is a towering figure of the post–New Negro Renaissance era. His autobiography *Black Boy* appears three years after Wright breaks with the Communist Party yet contains traces of his engagement with and critique of the Left and of modernism in both politics and aesthetics.

Wright's thoughts on Black urban life after the New Negro Movement prefaces Cayton and Drake's sociological masterpiece from which the epigraph to this chapter is taken. Wright identifies with the sociologists, explaining that all three of them lived their formative years in Chicago as a result of the Great Black Migration to the North to seek freedom and life in an effort he compares to the drama of the Greek theater and to Shakespeare's *Hamlet* (Cayton and Drake, xvii). As Wright expresses in his introduction to Cayton and Drake's book, "I did not know what my story was, and it was not until I stumbled upon science that I discovered some of the meanings of the environment that battered and taunted me" (ibid.). Wright describes the significance of scientific writing from "men" like Robert E. Park, Robert Redfield, and Louis Wirth as formative to his books *12,000 Back Voices, Native Son, Uncle Tom's Children,* and *Black Boy.* The "environment to which Negro boys and girls turn their eyes when they hear the word Freedom" corresponds to the Black metropolis described in Cayton and Drake's sociological work (xviii).

Wright's involvement with the CPUSA, his "Blueprint for Negro Art," and his "realist" protest fiction indicate what many consider to be key political and aesthetic questions of the period: what is the relationship between art and politics; how should the Black community be represented; and what role (symbolically and politically) do Black people play in the future of the nation and its vision of democracy? Looking at these debates from an intraracial vantage point challenges the logic of the "Negro problem," which objectifies Black people in order to mold them for assimilation. This dominant perspective on assimilation and integration evades the necessity to indict and transform a society structured by gendered racism.

Wright's attention to Black single mothers in *Black Boy*[14] (1945) already anticipates Moynihan's work by 30 years and centers intimate intraracial relations as formative to his political development and critique of the Left. Having migrated to Chicago, Wright portrays how he negotiated racism, segregation, and poverty by participating in predatory intraracial insurances schemes:

> I hungered for relief and, as a salesman of insurance to many young black girls, I found it. There were many young comely black housewives who, trying desperately to keep up their insurance payments, were willing to make bargains to escape paying a ten-cent premium. I had a long, tortured affair with one girl by paying her ten-cent premium each week. She was an illiterate black child with a baby whose father she did not know. During the entire period of my relationship with her, she had but one demand to make of me: She wanted me to take her to a circus. (276)

The personal relationships he establishes with these Black mothers parallels the relations of exploitation the insurance company devises to profit from Black poverty and marginalization. Even still, the details of her life, the absent father, and their torturous relationship

---

14. Richard Wright, *Black Boy (American Hunger): A Record of Childhood and Youth* (New York: Harper, 1945). Cited parenthetically throughout.

evoke the beginnings of Wright's own narrative and produce torment within him. "I could kill you," he says to the young woman, bringing his encounter with her to the brink of life and death (277). "Kill me, you said? You crazy, man," the woman replies (ibid.). Her reading of him positions her as a formidable antagonist, as "a human being to whom I could not talk" (ibid.). Wright's feelings of anger and insecurity in the presence of her humanity forces him to reconsider his own subject position, for he is angry with himself "for coming to her, hating my wild and restless loneliness" (ibid.). Wright takes part in the swindles of Black women as a means to stave off his own hunger, but he also recognizes his impotence against the Black owners of the burial societies "who were leaders in the Negro communities and were respected by whites" (280). His feelings of hunger and powerlessness compel his misogyny and his vile attitudes towards the victims of the company's schemes (ibid.).

Importantly, that feeling of torment and the pain that he carries from their intimate relationship moves him closer to witnessing her pain than the insurance scheme designed. In their intimate relations and through Wright's own narrative about a Black boy, the protagonist develops his revolutionary subjectivity through sharing these women's stories. It is in this same chapter that he describes encountering Communist speakers as he makes his rounds collecting money from Chicago's poor Black residents. Listening to their rhetoric, he recognizes a vast distance separating "the agitators from the masses, a distance so vast that the agitators did not know how to appeal to the people they sought to lead" (280). But in his criticism of the Communist speakers, doesn't Wright also accuse himself as duplicitous insurance agent and author of Black urban life?

The juxtaposition of his encounters with the poor Black mothers and with the agitators pushes him into closer alignment with Black people than with the Communist speakers: "I was now convinced that they did not know the complex nature of Negro life, did not know how great was the task to which they had set themselves" (283). Wright recognizes something, at this point ineffable, about the complex nature of Black life, but the remainder of *Black Boy* leads him towards the development of his revolutionary subjectivity and towards the task of writing or representing Black people: "I would hurl words into this darkness and wait for an echo . . . I would send other words to tell, to march, to fight, to create a sense of the hunger for life that gnaws in us all, to keep alive in our hearts a sense of the inexpressibly human" (365). Even still, in examining Wright's desire to write the revolution, we must ask how and why intraracial intimate antagonisms feature within the literature of the period. How do Black women's exploitation in *Black Boy* and Bessie's fatal brutalization in *Native Son* become necessary in narratives supposedly pushing for Black radicalism? Similarly, why do Himes's male protagonists demand Black women's subjection, even to the point of violence, in their struggles to come to terms with the call to activism?

To consider these questions, I turn to James Baldwin. In his critique of Wright, *Native Son,* and the genre of so-called protest fiction, Baldwin identifies the aesthetic and narrative absences of Black intersubjectivity as the flaw of such representations of Black life. In the essay "Many Thousands Gone,"[15] he writes:

> What this means for the novel is that a necessary dimension has been cut away; this dimension being the relationship that Negroes bear to one another, that depth of involvement and unspoken recognition of shared experience which creates a way of life. What the novel reflects—and at no point interprets—is the isolation of the Negro within his own group and the resulting fury of impatient scorn. It is this which creates its climate of anarchy and unmotivated and un-apprehended disaster; and it is this climate, common to most Negro protest novels, which has led us all to believe that in Negro life there exists no tradition, no field of manners, no possibility of ritual or intercourse, such as may, for example, sustain the Jew even after he has left his father's house. But the fact is not that the Negro has no tradition but that there has as yet arrived no sensibility sufficiently profound and tough to make this tradition articulate. (35)

By figuring White America's fantasy of Black manhood through the murderous character Bigger Thomas, readers, James Baldwin

---

15. Cited parenthetically throughout.

argues, never see into Black people's complex subjectivity. In fact, Bigger Thomas, as a reflection of White racist anxieties, is yielded no true consciousness of Black selfhood. In other words, he remains a bondsman to the lord's gaze. The concept of integration continues to fail within the project of assimilation.

But James Baldwin's preoccupation with Bigger Thomas ("Many Thousands Gone" is his second essay on the subject) does not lie primarily with the inherent constraints of the White racial gaze. In fact, the exclusive novelistic depiction of Black people in protest of White America's racial imaginary *excises* a necessary dimension of Black literature: "this dimension being the relationship that Negroes bear to one another" (27). For Baldwin, Black intimacy, seeing into and representing Black people's complex humanity, becomes visible not at the color line but behind the veil, or in the realm of Black interaction and intersubjectivity. Bigger Thomas *is* Baldwin's preoccupation and the antagonist of the possibility for seeing Black intimacy. "No American Negro exists," Baldwin continues, "who does not have his private Bigger Thomas living in the skull . . . what most significantly fails [*Native Son*] is the paradoxical adjustment which is perpetually made, the Negro being compelled to accept the fact that this dark and dangerous and unloved stranger is part of himself forever" (32).

Baldwin's preoccupation with Bigger Thomas is *both* about Black people's relationships to each other *and* about their relationships to themselves. The internal strife, the internal warring, the gap between how they are perceived and how they perceive, however, is *not* a gap to be closed or two halves to be merged. For Baldwin, recognizing the "Bigger within" is a "necessary ability to contain and even, in the most honorable sense of the word, to exploit the 'nigger,' which lends to Negro life its high element of the ironic and which causes the most well-meaning of the American critics to make such exhilarating errors when attempting to understand them" (33). Baldwin's description of the political and creative force of Black literature emphasizes the complexities within Black interiority.

Baldwin's first novel, *Go Tell It on the Mountain*[16] (1952), also provides a narrative of a Black boy coming into self-conscious man-

---

16. Cited parenthetically throughout.

hood, but the story comprises multiple characters' interiorities and self-reflections. Together, the novel incorporates these various subjects into a story about John Grimes's coming of age. "Everyone had always said that John would be a preacher when he grew up, just like his father," the novel begins. On the morning of his fourteenth birthday, the protagonist begins to think about this seemingly predetermined future and his own subject position distinct from but still in relation to his father Gabriel and his community. With "all the pressures of church and home uniting to drive him to the altar," John begins to reveal his anxiety about performing the role cast for him. Instead, he lives "for the day when his father would be dying and he, John, would curse him on his deathbed" (17). Because he sees his father as "the ambassador of the King of Heaven," he realizes that he could not "bow before the throne of grace without first kneeling to his father" (ibid.). Recognition of his father's power (as an extension of the Father's power) brings him to the precipice of life and death.

In John's world, the father's power is the immediate representation of authority. "Your daddy beats you . . . because he loves you," John's mother informs his brother Roy (21). The father wields patriarchal power over his family and religious rule seemingly ordained by God. Even still, the authoritative and even abusive power he wields over his household emerges from a distorted desire to love and protect his sons from racism. Gabriel teaches John that "all white people were wicked, and that God was going to bring them low" (39). Ironically, his father's religious and authoritarian teachings participate in socializing John to see himself as Bigger: "He, John, was a nigger, and he would find out, as soon as he got a little older, how evil white people could be" (40). Together with what John reads about lynching, unjust imprisonment, police violence, and labor discrimination, his father's imposition of love and fear educates him about his vulnerable position in the world. Fearing the father becomes a way to ensure his safety.

His feelings of vulnerability increase, however, at the scene of domestic violence. When John's brother Roy is stabbed during one of his forays onto the streets, the family argues over who is to blame for his injury. Addressing his wife, the father admonishes, "You can tell [Roy] to take this like a warning from the Lord. *This* is what white folks does to niggers" (54). Hurt by the father's seeming favoritism towards Roy over John, the mother responds, "*No*, I can't stop him, I done told you that, and you can't stop him neither. You don't know *what* to do with this boy, and that's why you all the time trying to fix the blame on somebody" (56). As the wife reveals the father's limited power and their son's vulnerability, the couple locks eyes in a moment of silent and agonizing recognition. Gabriel then reaches out "with all his might" and slaps Elizabeth, putting a violent end to their witnessing of each other's exposure and pain (57).

Baldwin's novel is no less attentive to the violent and material realities of racism than the so-called protest narratives. What *Go Tell It on the Mountain* emphasizes, however, are the complex ways that Black people negotiate oppression and community. "The Prayers of the Saints," part 2 of the novel, offers up prayer-narratives from Gabriel, his sister, Florence, and his wife, Elizabeth. In the setting of Gabriel's church, the congregation rises in musical unity, yet each member gives voice to her unique desire. When Aunt Florence is focalized in the narrative, for example, she recalls the lives of Black women, including her mother, a devout Christian born during slavery, and her neighbor Deborah, a sixteen-year-old raped by White men. Florence and Deborah become fast friends, sharing a hatred for all men, and developing their consciousness about the vulnerable position of Black women. Deborah's violation makes her "a living reproach, to herself and to all black women and to all black men" (91). She carries on her body the reminder of racist terror and the memory of her father's murder for attempting to avenge his daughter's violation. The lust that men feel towards Florence "could not be endured because it was so impersonal, limiting communion to the arc of shame" (ibid.). Black men's pursuit of self-conscious manhood requires communion with Black women and seeing them in their complex humanity. The two friends bond over shared understanding of the constraints on Black intimacy and its demand for mutual vulnerability.

Gabriel feels shame over his lustful desires. When he hears his sister Florence's cry in the church he is reminded of his own history, the painful loss of his mother, and her prayers over him. Gabriel remembers desperately trying to avoid his mother's and other women's gaze: "not looking at her, facing the mirror as he put on his jacket, and trying to avoid his face there, he told her that we was going to take a little walk" (120). His walks, however, lead him to the tavern and to the arms of multiple women. What Gabriel seems to realize, but is unwilling to confront, is the piercing recognition that would come from meeting Black women's gaze—a look that would force him to also see his own face, the one he even avoids in the mirror. His refusal to look at Black women this way fuels the shame around his sexual desire and leaves him divided against himself.

According to his public testimony, Gabriel's religious conversion allows him to see himself for the first time: "I looked at my hands and my hands were new. I looked at my feet and my feet were new. And I opened my mouth to the Lord that day and Hell won't make me change my mind" (125). This quoted monologue raises questions about the division between Gabriel's public performance as minister and his focalization in this section on his prayer. In other words, the narration of Gabriel's personal prayer mimics the division he experiences in his own subjectivity. Although he takes Deborah as a wife due to her pious and long-suffering appearance, she never calls him "Gabriel or 'Gabe,' but from the time that he began to preach she called him Reverend" (127–28). Gabriel still clings to what he and Deborah represented to the community: "She, who had been the living proof and witness of their daily shame, and who had become their holy fool—and he, who had been the untamable despoiler of their daughters, and thief of their women, their walking prince of darkness!" (143). His marriage to Deborah and his role as preacher become ways for him to negotiate the Bigger within.

The tensions that John, Florence, Gabriel, and Elizabeth experience inform our reading of John's coming-of-age. Similar to Wright's project to become a witness for Black people's living, Baldwin constructs a narrative wherein Black intersubjectivity is both witnessed and lived. The prayers of the saints inform and provoke John's experience on the "threshing-floor" and bring him to depart from his father's path.

The meaning of integration in this era of activism emphasizes the complexity of and shifting representations of Black subjectivity. Although the Communist Party, as Richard Iton argues, "established closer links with the civil rights movement than any other progressive movement in American history," its inability to deal with Black autonomy and its shifting attitude towards the civil rights cause made the CPUSA less than an ideal partner.[17] The NAACP's and the civil rights movement's reluctance to appear anti-American also complicated the necessary critique of racism domestically and attachments to anticolonial energies abroad.[18] African American literature's unique conception of integration as it relates to Black interiority and subjectivity refracts this paradox while prioritizing intraracial relations as the site for imagining Black people's place in the United States and in the world. Black women writers extend these priorities and reconceive the temporalities of nation and activism through their portrayals of intimate antagonisms.

THE INTIMATE REPRESENTATION OF FAMILIAL FRAGMENTATION

> *For me, writing was an act of love. It was an attempt—not to get the world's attention—it was an attempt to be loved. It seemed a way to save myself and to save my family.*
>
> —James Baldwin

Baldwin describes writing as an act of love and salvation for himself and his family. Intimate antagonisms in Baldwin's work further elucidate the importance of writing through conflict as a process of intimate struggle and reconciliation for Black subjects. Apart from revolutionary struggles, another site for contemplating subjectivity and consciousness during this period is within the portrayal of Black family relations. Given the close connection between the conception of community and the representation of family, African American literature during the postwar era features complex portrayals of the Black family. Intimate representations of familial conflict reconfigure dominant debates about integration and racial equality. These depic-

---

17. Richard Iton, *In Search of the Black Fantastic: Politics and Popular Culture in the Post-Civil Rights Era* (Oxford; New York: Oxford University Press, 2008), 33.

18. Ibid., 39.

tions still recognize the imposition of anti-Black racism and racial capitalism, but center intraracial relations in all of their complexity. Black writers attentive to the intersections of race, class, gender, and sexuality again come to the forefront as they challenge the dominant meanings of life and integration in the post–Negro Renaissance era. Rather than the decisiveness of violent action, Black women's time, the moments of the everyday and the intimate, becomes a vehicle through which these productive tensions can be explored.

In distinction to the lynching dramas of the late nineteenth and early twentieth centuries that Koritha Mitchell[19] describes, depictions of Black domestic life in the post–World War II era make the living rooms, bedrooms, and kitchens of Black homes the setting to explore the complex relationships Black people have to each other and to themselves in the everyday realities of Black life. Gwendolyn Brooks is one author of the post–Negro Renaissance period who reimagines questions about Black intimacy and Black integration through representations of the Black family. Intimate, familial antagonisms also structure works like Paule Marshall's *Brown Girl, Brownstones* (1959), Dorothy West's *The Living Is Easy* (1948), James Baldwin's *Go Tell It on the Mountain* (1953), and Lorraine Hansberry's *Raisin in the Sun* (1959). For Black women writers like Brooks, examining the complexities of Black motherhood provided a venue for the contemplation of integration and double consciousness. Decades after the advent of the Black women's club movement[20] and with the ongoing improvement societies' enabling of the transition of Black migrants to the city,[21] the discussion of Black motherhood as well as its discontents offered an important literary site for examining Black experience in the (post) World War II era. Anxieties about prostitution and the dangers for single women considering the lures of urban life contributed to the public discourse about Black female sexuality and the

---

19. See Koritha Mitchell, *Living with Lynching: African American Lynching Plays, Performance, and Citizenship, 1890–1930* (Urbana: University of Illinois Press, 2011).

20. See Evelyn Brooks Higginbotham, *Righteous Discontent: The Women's Movement in the Black Baptist Church, 1880–1920* (Cambridge, MA: Harvard University Press, 1993).

21. See Hazel Carby, "Policing the Black Woman's Body in an Urban Context," *Critical Inquiry* 18.4 (Summer 1992): 738–55.

sacredness of traditional forms of domesticity.[22] Yet Brooks writes precisely about the failures in the context of Black intimate relations.

Brooks's prose fiction work *Maud Martha*[23] (1953) portrays the eponymous protagonist's maturation and socialization from childhood, to marriage, and motherhood. Spanning the periods before, during, and after World War II, the novel offers an invaluable point of view on the radical imaginary informing civil rights debates about integration and community. "On her way back down the squeezing dark of the hall she felt—something softly separate in her," the narrator describes at the beginning of the chapter unceremoniously titled "a birth" (89). Depicting Maud Martha's labor and delivery, the chapter reports the dialogue between the expectant mother and her husband, Paul. The narrator, however, alters focalization between the two parents and their respective anxieties about impending parenthood. The feeling of "something softly separate" within Maud Martha, therefore, is mimicked in the narration of her childbirth. "She began to whimper in a manner that made Paul want to vomit. His thoughts traveled to the girl he had met at the Dawn Ball several months before. Cool. Sweet. Well-groomed. Fair" (91–92), the narrator conveys to the reader about Paul's inner thoughts. "He walked about the room several times. He went to the dresser and began to brush his hair. She looked at him in speechless contempt," Maud Martha seethes, as her labor pains intensify (92).

Black motherhood and sexuality represent double consciousness par excellence. As Darlene Clark Hine describes, a gendered perspective on double consciousness multiplies the possibilities for interpreting the levels of consciousness that comprise African American life and experience, as well as the ideas and strategies for expanding the Black radical imagination.[24] Brooks's writing on Black motherhood and domesticity incorporates such a notion of consciousness as individual and communal. The post–Negro Renaissance era extends

---

22. See Jenkins, *Private Lives, Proper Relations*.
23. Cited parenthetically throughout.
24. Darlene Clark Hine, "'In the Kingdom of Culture': Black Women and the Intersection of Race, Gender, and Class," in *Lure and Loathing: Essays on Race, Identity, and the Ambivalence of Assimilation,* edited by Gerald Early (New York: Allen Lane; Penguin, 1993), 337–51.

the literary depiction of the Black family as a metaphor for the community. In distinction to the lynching dramas from the period 1890–1930[25] that portray the Black family as normative, coherent, vibrant, and loving, the representations emerging from the long civil rights era figure the Black family as a locus for intimate antagonisms.

The birth of Paul and Maud Martha's daughter Paulette reveals the intimate antagonisms that pervade the entire novel. The girl Paul previously meets at the Dawn Ball, for example, is described in the chapter titled "if you're light and have long hair." "At the Ball, there will only be beautiful girls, or real stylish ones. There won't be more than a handful like me," Maud Martha contemplates, as she peruses the invitation to the dance (81). That her husband leaves her sitting alone "trying not to feel the inferiority that she did not feel" while he dances with a curvy, attractive woman who is "white as a white" contributes to Maud Martha's sense of undesirability and invisibility. These feelings emerge early in her life within her own family. Maud Martha's younger sister, Helen, is the fairer of the two and the beauty that reduces Martha to just an "old black gal" in the eyes of the young men who evaluate and dismiss her so swiftly (34). What's more, Maud Martha espies her low ranking not only in the perspective of potential suitors "but even with their father—their mother—their brother" (35). Attitudes about fair skin, beauty, and value lead Maud Martha to choose Paul as her husband, although she cautions him about her inability to reproduce for him beautiful children. "I am not a pretty woman," she warns him; "if you married a pretty woman, you could be the father of beautiful children" (54). Priding himself on his fair skin, Paul laments his "real Negro features" (ibid.). Silently, Maud Martha accepts that "there would be little 'beauty' getting born out of such a union" (ibid.). Thus Paulette's birth unleashes for Paul the lost possibility of reproducing "beauty" understood as fair skin. Maud Martha, looking with speechless contempt at Paul on the verge of fatherhood, recalls a long history of hurts and resentment.

The birthing process of becoming two instantiates a doubling (tripling?) of consciousness. The quoted dialogue and unspoken

---

25. Mitchell, *Living with Lynching*.

thoughts between Paul and Maud Martha also reveal the potential proliferation of consciousness about the terms of beauty and desire. Colorism, the social assignment of increasing value based on skin color among racially subordinated communities, indicates how prejudices about skin color emerge from White supremacy. But what affect lies behind such color consciousness? The feelings of value, worth, value, belonging, and desirability are unlimited in their significance, yet the terms left to Black people to represent them leave them fighting over the remnants and fragments of beauty. If they could be redefined, what other memories, affects, possibilities, and language could be too? How might these terms provoke new forms of belonging, community, and intimacy?

Brooks's novel rejects the demands for sameness or alignment with the dominant ideals for belonging and integration rooted in White supremacy. Maud Martha imagines these possibilities through the relationships she establishes with the "kitchenette folks" who live with and beside her. Her neighbors in nontraditional and even interracial domestic arrangements become representative of a new set of communal relations and cohesion. And as the novel concludes, with Black soldiers returning from war, she anticipates the spirit of the civil rights movement: "while people did live they would be grand, would be glorious and brave, would have nimble hearts that would beat and beat. . . . And, in the meantime, she was going to have another baby" (179–80).

In addition to narratives about motherhood, the very representation of Black intimate and domestic space also figures prominently in interrogation of integration in scenes of interpersonal violence. Ann Petry's short story "Like a Winding Sheet" (1945)[26] depicts the domestic and professional lives of Mae and her unnamed husband. The demands and degradations of their workplaces regularly interrupt the couple's domestic interactions. The story opens with the pair awaking and contemplating breakfast: "He had planned to get up before Mae did and surprise her by fixing breakfast. Instead he went back to sleep and she got out of bed so quietly he didn't know she wasn't there beside him" (1497). The careful consideration the couple

---

26. Cited parenthetically throughout.

demonstrates collides with the stresses and strains of low-wage labor: "'Today's payday. And payday is a good luck day everywhere any way you look at it.' . . . And he was late for work again because they spent fifteen minutes arguing before he could convince her she ought to go to work just the same" (1498). He speaks to her "persuasively" rather than "roughly." The narrator's report of his inner thoughts reveals to the reader his refusal to "threaten to strike her like a lot of men might have done" (1499). Although he considers himself above other men in that regard, the seemingly passing thought foreshadows the story's tragic conclusion.

It is his White female "foreman," Mrs. Scott, who becomes the fantasied repository for his frustrations and growing rage. When Mrs. Scott confronts him about his tardiness, she completely disregards his complaint about the ache in his legs: "Excuses. . . . And the niggers are the worst. I don't care what's with your legs. You get in here on time. I'm sick of you niggers—" (1499). Challenging her for the racial epithet, he steps closer to her, clenching his fists. Although Mrs. Scott backs down, he relishes the pleasure of the fantasy of his fists pummeling her soft face: "his hands were not exactly a part of him anymore—they had developed a separate life of their own over which he had no control. So he dwelt on the pleasure his hands would have felt" (1500). Again reminding himself that he cannot strike a woman, his thoughts continue to alternate between satisfying his rage and remembering his nonversion of masculinity.

At home for dinner, Mae prepares a meal and invites him to eat. Giggling and coaxing him to dine, she sarcastically jokes, "You're nothing but a old hungry nigger trying to act tough and—" (1503). Realizing the error in her ribbing, Mae pauses. The narrator intervenes and brings the story to its conclusion. "She was standing close to him and that funny tingling started in his finger tips, went fast up his arms and sent his fist shooting straight for her face. There was the smacking sound of soft flesh being struck by a hard object and it wasn't until she screamed that he realized he had hit her in the mouth" (ibid.). "Like a Winding Sheet" ends, somewhat, like it begins—with the narration of Mae and her husband at home. The winding sheet that wraps her husband in their marriage bed, however, becomes a symbol of the feelings of strangulation that brings the narrative to its violent conclusion. Mae's use of the n-word epithet and her gendered location bring her into too close proximity with the female "foreman" who denigrates Mae's husband at work. Yet the racial distance between the "foreman" and Mae enables her husband to unleash his rage and aggression.

We have seen in the works of Himes and Wright how the demands of labor and of domestic life intertwine in the portrayals of intraracial, intimate antagonisms. Petry's short story depicts how the putatively lonely crusade marked out by Black men already indicates the severing of communal bonds and intimacies that foster the hope for transformation and justice. In his efforts to triumph over the imposition of inferiority and servility, the husband's violent encounter with his wife projects onto her the death over which he so desperately wishes to gain mastery. As Tricia Rose argues, "intimate relationships are never privately negotiated; they are defined significantly by complex public discourses, policies, and institutions."[27] While these discourses and policies impact intraracial intimacies, these Black women writers also give attention to the political consciousness that is either developed or suffocated in the interpersonal relations where freedom dreams and revolutionary subjectivity are shared and fostered.[28] Black consciousness, therefore, does not simply reject the division between the public and private spheres but connects intraracial intimacies and Black intersubjectivity to a more radical conception of Black integration.

---

27. Rose, "Hansberry's *A Raisin in the Sun*," 31.
28. Ibid., 33.

CHAPTER 3

Going to Bed Angry

Intimate Antagonisms in the Epoch of Black Power

THE PUBLIC DEBATE between Black men and women over the representation of racist oppression may be the most important example of the significance and complexity bearing on intimate antagonism. The publication and mainstream attention garnered by fictional works like Toni Morrison's *The Bluest Eye* (1970), Gayl Jones's *Corregidora* (1975), Ntozake Shange's *for colored girls* (1975), and Alice Walker's *The Color Purple* (1982) challenged readers' conceptions of racism during the transition to the post–civil rights era. By depicting intraracial child abuse, incest, rape, and domestic violence, these creative texts risked seeming to be in alliance with dominant notions about the pathological Black family as they attempted to account for the interlocking relationships between racist and gendered forms of domination. Such portrayals of intraracial violence frustrated the singular representation of Black men as victims of oppression and proved the divide between the public sphere and intimate dynamics to be false. The intensity of the critiques against these Black women writers and their works, and the longevity of the intraracial debate about gender and racism, reveal the significant degree to which the politics of intimate antagonism figure in discussions about antiracist struggle, contemporary Black subjectivity, community formation, and cultural production.

Most analyses of the debate about the public portrayals of intraracial conflict converge on masculinist ideologies associated with familial norms. The betrayal of the communal pact to portray only positive images of Black people, the revelation of family secrets, and the daughter's struggle to wrest narrative control from an authoritative father were unspoken expectations about the form and function of African American cultural texts. The public debate played out in the terms of familial drama and betrayal. Chief among these analyses is Deborah McDowell's "Reading Family Matters," wherein she discusses how the Black family comes to represent a totalizing fiction employed to ameliorate the painful and complex past of racial oppression. Recognizing Black men as the patriarchs of a traditional family would seemingly complete the trajectory from bondage to freedom. Hetero-patriarchal familial relations provide the basis for recognizing the Black nuclear family and Black masculinity and femininity as normative. Such normative forms of recognition are deeply connected to the belief in the traditional nuclear family as a pillar of society.

The fictional representation of the sexual violation of kinship structure introduces an unsettling gender consciousness into the struggle for racial inclusion and equality. Black women's claims about intraracial sexual violence rattle the foundations upon which Black men sought civic inclusion as patriarchs. Such a Black feminist challenge also rendered intraracial, intragender recognition a salient factor in antiracist discourses. Black women's novels that contextualize the scene of incest within the brutalities of persistent racism and de facto segregation explore how structural conditions of disenfranchisement also provoke intraracial fracturing. Southern segregation, the urban ghetto, the shrinking welfare state, and the pathologization of Black maternity create conditions that render Black women vulnerable, unprotected, and seemingly "worthy" of their oppression. In contrast, the depiction of intraracial sexual violence is aimed at the investment in the dominant terms for defining masculinity, and the desire for racial equality on the basis of patriarchal privilege. The cost of inclusion, of recognition, within such a system of profound racial and gender inequality requires Black women's degradation and submission.

An exclusive focus on Black Power and the public debate between Black women writers and Black male critics can also evade the structural forces of that historical moment and their impact on how Black people represented themselves in fiction and to each other. Already in the late 1960s, Richard Nixon's presidency worked very hard to reverse the gains, momentum, and sentiment produced by civil rights activism. His focus on dismantling welfare and on law and order redeployed images of Black people as criminal, lazy, promiscuous, and parasitic.[1] The intensification of such derogatory images and the federally sanctioned abandonment of poor Black peoples in the 1980s are important historical events that unfold in the same era as the debate over some Black women's fiction. Why, in a moment of danger, of provisional victory, and of continued assault on Black people's position in U.S. politics and society, would some Black women say "no" to Black men? What were their visions of liberation that some would not go along with a view of equality rooted in a traditional form of patriarchy that disavows the persistence of intraracial sexual violence in the past and present?

Note that Black women's creative writing was the principal, public site where the debate over the representation of Black life occurred. Black women's literature becomes an important site for portraying the intergenerational legacy of racial and gendered violence. Contending with the histories of violence and exploitation produces intraracial conflicts in African American women's novels as their characters struggle to come to terms with how these legacies of oppression shape intimate antagonisms. Especially in the domain of racialized gender, grappling with the complex history of abuse persists as an important dimension of intimate antagonism.

---

1. Linda Faye Williams, *The Constraint of Race: Legacies of White Skin Privilege in America* (University Park: Pennsylvania State University Press, 2003), 173.

INTIMATE ANTAGONISM AND THE NEO-SLAVE NARRATIVE

> When I'm telling you something don't you ever ask if I'm lying. Because they didn't want to leave no evidence of what they done—so it couldn't be held against them. And I'm leaving evidence. And you got to leave evidence too. And your children got to leave evidence. And when it come time to hold up the evidence, we got to have evidence to hold up. That's why they burned all the papers, so there wouldn't be no evidence to hold up against them.
>
> —Gayl Jones, *Corregidora*

This charge to her great-granddaughter, about holding up the evidence of systematic racist and sexual violence, sets the stage for a series of intimate antagonisms in Gayl Jones's novel *Corregidora*.[2] In it, the protagonist Ursa must revisit the past sexual abuse that the Brazilian slave-owner, sex broker, and patriarch Corregidora inflicts on her female ancestors. "Holding up evidence," as Great Gram describes, is no simple project. Great Gram demands that Ursa Corregidora (and all the Corregidora women) leave evidence of the incestuous, interracial sexual violence suffered under slavery. The commitment of succeeding generations to tell that story (and presumably their own) would confirm Great Gram's oral history and experiences. "And when it come time," the cumulative remembering and retelling, Great Gram implies, would make justice possible—or at least an alternative to the continued degradation of Black women. Alternatives don't always come easily. Great Gram testifies to the power of an alternative knowledge structure that is both intergenerational and collective. Yet the cost of maintaining the evidence needed for justice requires collective, constant remembering, and regular communion with a history of degradation. Within Great Gram's schema, the "scar that's left to bear witness" becomes the embodied identification of a politicized Black womanhood "as visible as our blood" (72).

---

2. Cited parenthetically throughout.

Holding up evidence in the novel refers as much to the silencing of crucial testimony that Black subjects need in the struggle for racial justice as it does to the radical act of bearing witness to the historical and political significance of Black women's sexual violation. Sexual violation is a key mechanism through which racial subordination was implemented. It represents a doubly effective form of suppression because it both humiliates and blames the victim. Great Gram insists that Black women leave evidence because any official, incriminating evidence against the dominant was burned (9). Her demand reveals the understanding that Black women do not control the hegemonic production of meaning and knowledge. Dominant, official histories of slavery disavow the systematic abuse of Black women. How could White patriarchy justify its "right" to power and acknowledge the torture, rape, and destruction of Black women's bodies upon which such power depended? Recognizing the (White power structure's) systematic refusal of Black women's evidence and of their testimonies, Great Gram anticipates a *future* opportunity for justice that requires remembering Black people's collective racial *past*.

Throughout the novel, the "present" represents the very intersection between the past and future. More specifically, how Black men and women remember that past shapes future aspirations for justice from the vantage point of present struggles. Black men also need this remembering, for it is not merely the personal and parochial experience of Black women. In tandem with the spectacular torture and murder of Black men through lynching, the violation of Black women is also an exercise of White male authority and power. As Gerda Lerner argues, the rape of Black women also demonstrated Black males' lack of power, for they were symbolically castrated in their inability to defend Black women and lynched for associating with White women. Therefore, Black women were doubly instrumentalized as objects of forcible rape and as instruments in the degradation of Black men.[3] The sexual assault of Black women forms part of the reinforcing structure upholding a system of racial

---

3. Gerda Lerner, *Black Women in White America: A Documentary History* (1972; New York: Pantheon Books, 1992).

and economic exploitation. *Corregidora* portrays how the wounding that Blacks have suffered collectively plays out in the most intimate realms of intraracial life and relationships. Ursa's partner Mutt, his physical attacks on her, and her resultant miscarriage instigate her reassessment of her responsibility to historical revision because the patterns of the past persist in the present and impede progress toward the future. Significantly, such critical reassessment does not *only* occur at the "color line" but rather in the realms of intimate antagonism between African Americans as well.

"It was 1947 when Mutt and I was married," Ursa states at the opening of the novel, positioning her oral narrative as the most recent expression of evidence stemming from Great Gram's history (3). In that same paragraph, the protagonist informs us that in 1948 her jealous husband stormed into Happy's Café where she worked as a blues singer. Enraged by the gaze that male spectators cast over the songstress (the way "they mess with they eyes"), an intoxicated Mutt attempts to reassert his threatened authority and ownership over Ursa. "That was when I fell," she recounts, and then goes on to explain how this fall results in the loss of her womb through an emergency hysterectomy. The novel's present is the story of Ursa's fall and her process of healing. The space of intimate antagonism organizes temporality and creates a collective site for conflict and articulating the desire for remedy.

Although summarily stated at the outset of the novel, Mutt's abuse, Ursa's desire to sing, and her "fall" activate Ursa's recognition of the obligation to leave evidence. Processing the pain of Mutt's abuse and the resultant loss of her ability to become a mother, Ursa initially struggles to reconcile her current plight with her maternal ancestors' histories:

> My great-grandmama told my grandmamma the part she lived through that my grandmamma didn't live through and my grandmamma told my mama what they both lived through and my mama told me what they all lived through and we were suppose to pass it down like that from generation to generation so we'd never forget. Even though they'd burned everything to play like it didn't never happen. Yeah, and where's the next generation? (9)

In this passage Ursa's language rushes together as she explains the imbrications of oral narratives and experiences that join her ancestors together. Their unity in narrative also counters the hegemony of the incestuous link between them engendered by Corregidora's sexual violation of Great Gram's offspring. The final two sentences that reference the official strategies for recognizing and destroying evidence, and the intimate conflict that prohibits Ursa from testifying, interrupt the fluid description of the intersubjective relations between the Corregidora women. Mutt's violence against Ursa symbolizes the impossibility of her motherhood, and his refusal to acknowledge why the Corregidora women privilege the "womb" as the site and source for carrying the history of racial subjugation. Although Ursa seems unaware at the outset of the novel, her narrative efforts to process her loss and her ancestors' experiences *do* grant her a mode for bearing witness and leaving evidence. The claims that the past (and future) has on the present, what Walter Benjamin calls "the secret agreement between past generations and the present one,"[4] and Ursa's need to wrestle with the past in order to establish alternative possibilities for the future situate *Corregidora* firmly within the neo-slave narrative genre.

INTIMATE TRAUMA AND HISTORICAL LEGACIES

How we imagine our collective past matters significantly to how we interpret our present struggles and envision a more just future. The neo-slave narrative is one key Black[5] literary site where intimate antagonisms emerge and challenge our understandings of resistance. Given that Black women and men have been forced closer

---

4. Walter Benjamin, "Theses on the Philosophy of History," in *Illuminations*, edited and introduced by Hannah Ahrendt (New York: Schocken Books, 1968), 254.

5. I use the term *Black* in the context of the neo-slave narrative because they also appear in other national contexts like Cuba during the 1960s. The histories of the "triangular trade," structures of racial oppression, and the significance of revolutionary thought and activism partially account for the neo-slave narrative's transnational popularity during the so-called turbulent '60s. See, for example, Esteban Montejo / Miguel Barnet, *Autobiografia de un Cimarron / Autobiography of a Runaway Slave* (Willimantic, CT: Curbstone Books, 1966).

together because of racism, it may not be surprising that sometimes they would be at each other's throats.[6] Ashraf Rushdy, in *Neo-Slave Narratives: Studies in the Social Logic of a Literary Form*, argues that the neo-slave narrative has "its origins in the social, intellectual, and racial formations of the sixties," and describes how "these texts intervene in debates over the significance of race."[7] Literary revisions of slavery challenge readers to come to terms with the *ongoing* pursuit of racial justice, rejecting the notion that matters of racial inequality no longer construct contemporary realities. The emergence of the neo-slave narrative genre in the turbulent 1960s reflects the dominant literary interpretation of those texts as contesting the betrayals of democracy and human justice *despite* civil rights gains and Black Power activism. Four key themes persist in critical analyses of the neo-slave narrative's form and historical development. The genre focuses on the betrayals of "freedom" and the continued refusal of Black Americans' full inclusion and efforts at self-assertion in the 1960s and 1970s.[8] The neo-slave narrative interrogates the emancipatory promise of print literacy, a central premise of the nineteenth-century slave narrative and its role in the pursuit of political and social recognition.[9] In its visionary aspects the neo-slave narrative explores postmodern forms of freedom, family, and community.[10] Finally, the genre rewrites slave history in contestation of the dominant, national accounts of the antebellum period that imagined slaves as docile, compliant, submissive, and content.

Analyses of the neo-slave narrative rightfully address how neoconservative viciousness and unrelenting poverty impacted the attitudes and conventions of African American novelists during the

---

6. See Cornel West and bell hooks, *Breaking Bread* (Boston: South End Press, 1991).

7. Ashraf H. A. Rushdy, *Neo-Slave Narratives: Studies in the Social Logic of a Literary Form* (New York: Oxford University Press, 1997), 3.

8. See Bernard Bell, *The Afro American Novel and Its Tradition* (Amherst: University of Massachusetts Press, 1987), and Rushdy, *Neo-Slave Narratives*.

9. Madhu Dubey, "The Politics of Genre in *Beloved*," *NOVEL: A Forum on Fiction* 32.2 (Spring 1999): 187–206.

10. Timothy A. Spaulding, *Re-Forming the Past: History, the Fantastic, and the Postmodern Slave Narrative* (Columbus: The Ohio State University Press, 2005).

post–civil rights era.[11] Many of these analyses, however, focus on Black male political culture, gender normativity, and heteropatriarchy in response to the racist portrayals of the enslaved. For example, a key contestation of the neo-slave narrative emerges in imagining what kind of slave existed on the plantation with regard to gender normativity, traditional family formation, and oppositional consciousness.[12] Rereadings of slavery were explicitly gendered. These authoritative revisions of slavery envisioned Black men and women as nonnormative—albeit a nonnormativity that the plantation regime produced. Scholars like Stanley Elkins and Daniel Patrick Moynihan, for example, presented research defending the thesis of putative "black male dependency" and infantilization.[13] Because the slave-owner's power was emphasized in their analyses, the Black man as "Sambo," docile, lazy, and irresponsible, was reified as the real product of slavery. Rendering the Black male childlike and power-

---

11. Anti-busing campaigns, the weakening or cutting of civil rights programs and activities, tax relief for the wealthiest Americans, the "war on drugs," the rapid development of the prison industrial complex, and the shrinking welfare state are some of the setbacks that scholars examine in characterizing the challenges to freedom and equality in the post–civil rights era. See George Lipsitz, *The Possessive Investment in Whiteness: How White People Profit from Identity Politics* (Philadelphia: Temple University Press, 1998); Ruth Wilson Gilmore, *Golden Gulag*; Tricia Rose, *Black Noise: Rap Music and Black Culture in Contemporary America* (Hanover, NH: Wesleyan University Press, 1994); Mike Davis, *City of Quartz: Excavating the Future in Los Angeles* (New York: Vintage Books, 1992); and Robin D. G. Kelley, *Yo Mama's Dysfunktional: Fighting the Culture Wars in Urban America* (Boston: Beacon, 1997).

12. See, for example, Daniel Patrick Moynihan and the U.S. Department of Labor, *The Negro Family: The Case for National Action* (Washington, DC: USGPO, 1965); John Blassingame, *The Slave Community: Plantation Life in the Antebellum South* (New York: Oxford University Press, 1972); and Herbert Gutman, *The Black Family in Slavery and Freedom, 1750–1925* (New York: Pantheon Books, 1976).

13. Stanley Elkins, *Slavery: A Problem in American Institutional and Intellectual Life* (Chicago: University of Chicago Press, 1976); Moynihan, "The Negro Family: The Case for National Action." There are numerous critical responses and revisionist histories to Elkins's and Moynihan's scholarship, including Blassingame, *The Slave Community*, and Gutman, *The Black Family in Slavery and Freedom, 1750–1925*. Black feminist responses are also copious, including analyses by Hortense Spillers, "Mama's Baby, Papa's Maybe," and Angela Davis, "Reflections on the Black Woman's Role in the Community of Slaves," in *The Angela Davis Reader* (Malden, MA: Blackwell, 1998), 111–28.

less, the Black female, according to this scholarship, assumed a larger role in the Black family, and further hindered the very possibility of Black patriarchy. Black male rereadings of slavery during the Black Power era (and beyond) therefore inscribed an insurgent enslaved male on the plantation site.[14] This figure was described as possessing the patriarchal characteristics necessary for the recognition of Black masculinity and outsmarting the machinations of White patriarchal authority.

While both hegemonic *and* counterhegemonic reinterpretations of slavery attempted to describe the slave in light of the social and political challenges of the 1960s, scholars and even state-appointed commissions attributed urban riots, Black poverty, unemployment, and spatial isolation and segregation in the ghettos of virtually every American city to the persistence of racial discrimination.[15] Nevertheless, theories that defined and therefore produced the "black urban underclass" argued that Black disadvantage stemmed from the degeneracy of Black culture generally, and from Black people's inability to perform socially recognizable gender roles. Rather than evaluating the abuses of power and continued structural inequality, theories traced the cause of Black Americans' inferior social, political, and economic position ideologically to nonconformity to traditional gender roles.

The material constraints and discursive limits that racism establishes do impact the neo-slave narrative genre. But such exclusive analytic focus on anti-Black racism, instead of attention to *gendered racism,* enables us only to imagine conceptions of resistance, freedom, healing, and pleasure as remedies to conflicts derived at the "color-line" and in the service of establishing Black desires for heteronormativity as the underlying motivation for resistance strat-

---

14. See, for examples, Ishmael Reed, *Flight to Canada* (New York: Random House, 1976), and Rushdy, *Neo-Slave Narratives.*

15. See for examples, *Violence in the City: An End or a Beginning? A Report by the Governor's Commission on the Los Angeles Riots* (CA: Governor's Commission on the Los Angeles Riots, 1965); the *Report of the National Advisory Commission on Civil Disorders* [The Kerner Report] (Washington, DC: U.S. National Advisory Commission on Civil Disorders, 1968); and Douglas S. Massey and Nancy A. Denton, *American Apartheid: Segregation and the Making of the Underclass* (Cambridge: Harvard University Press, 1993).

egies. Black women's testimonies of sexual violence thus seem like a betrayal of male modernist notions of freedom. As Angela Davis points out, dominant narratives of slavery grossly distort the lens for examining Black women's lives and experiences. Davis's seminal essay and reevaluation of enslaved women's role in the community of slaves also calls for a critical consideration of intraracial negotiations.[16] Likewise, *Corregidora*'s display of intimate antagonism prioritizes the process through which Black people negotiate over the meaning of their collective racial history and their current struggles for justice. What demands further analysis is why the expression of Black women's experiences of racialized sexual violence in particular provoked a crisis within antiracist discourse during the late twentieth century about how racism itself was understood and therefore struggled against during the height of civil rights and Black Power antiracist movements and their legacies. A central area of struggle over the gendered, sexual representation of the enslaved is the painful issue of sexual violence and coercion. One reason sexual violence incites such a strong response is that it raises issues about nonnormativity and the bases for inclusion and recognition. The recurring depiction of racialized, sexual brutality, and the struggle to "bear witness" to that narrative, points to an unresolved collective trauma that both Black men and women grappled with during the civil rights and Black Power eras.

In *The Afro-American Novel and Its Tradition*, Bernard Bell presents a survey of African American literature and describes the distinctive features of this literary tradition. Bell coins the term "neoslave narrative" in this text, and provides a basic working definition of this genre: "residually oral, modern narratives of escape from bondage to freedom."[17] Bell situates the development of this modern form within the disappointments, setbacks, and renegotiations that characterize the post–civil rights era. Although he does not cite Bell's

---

16. George Rawick and Cedric Robinson also show resistance as a central activity of enslaved Africans and a group exercise of agency grounded in collective forms of resistance. Rawick, *From Sunup to Sundown*; Robinson, *Black Marxism*; Angela Davis, "Reflections on the Black Woman's Role in the Community of Slaves," *Black Scholar* 3 (December 1971): 2–16.

17. Bell, *The Afro-American Novel and Its Tradition*, 289.

text, Ashraf H. A. Rushdy also provides a definition of the "Neo-slave narrative": "contemporary novels that assume the form, adopt the conventions, and take on the first-person voice of the antebellum slave narrative."[18] Rushdy adds that these narratives also "cite" the historical moment from which they emerge and further explores the origins of these texts in the social, intellectual, political, and cultural climate of the 1960s. He examines, in great detail, the dialogue he considers authors of the neo-slave narrative to be having with the legacy and impact of the Black Power era. For Rushdy and Bell, political forces and social conditions shape the field of cultural production out of which this genre of historical fiction appears. However, despite the fact that his periodization of the neo-slave narrative depends on the rise of Black Power and New Left social history between 1966 and 1968, Rushdy claims Ernest Gaines's *The Autobiography of Miss Jane Pittman* (1971), not *Jubilee* (1966), as the first in this genre.[19] *Jubilee*[20] narrates the African American experience of the slavery, the Civil War, and Reconstruction through "its female line of spiritual descent."[21] Walker's neo-slave narrative centralizes the Black female ancestors through the perspective of the central character Vyry. *Jubilee* opens with the passing of Vyry's mother, Sis Hetta, in childbirth. Sis Hetta, we learn, has been claimed as the "Marster's woman," birthed fifteen children, and has been given Jake for a husband. Jake "hated Marster and despised himself and looked at Hetta and got mad and evil" (15). Jake's uncertainties about his or his child's fate once Sis Hetta dies in *Jubilee*'s gender-specific neo-slave narrative reveal the importance of Black women's experiences and position to the community as a whole. Walker's text also situates the sexual violation and degradation of Black women as a foundational aspect of slavery's legacy.

Gaines's important work *The Autobiography of Miss Jane Pittman* features the first-person narrative of Miss Pittman, and spans from the 1860s to the 1960s, from slavery to civil rights. This narrative

---

18. Rushdy, *Neo-Slave Narratives*, 3.
19. Ibid., 3–6.
20. Cited parenthetically throughout.
21. Hortense Spillers, "A Hateful Passion, a Lost Love: Three Women's Fiction" (1983), in Spillers, *Black, White, and in Color*, 104.

portrays the physical violence and threat of death intended to thwart Black struggles for self-determination. The character Jane Pittman therefore symbolizes the resoluteness and righteousness of the African American pursuit of liberation and equality. But is recognition of Pittman's political subjectivity understood in terms of her raced *and* gendered locations? *The Autobiography* conforms its eponymous Black female narrator to the demand of resistance to state power and racism. Such a conception of resistance aligns with the modern civil rights movement's definition of manhood and its association with political inclusion.[22] Both the concerns about economic inequity (which determines social and political status, political voice, one's position as head of household and primary breadwinner), and access to resources (which shapes one's impact on the public sphere and control over other individuals) attached manhood to political and racial justice. Thus, when the White southerner Tee Bob commits suicide because he cannot marry a Creole woman in *The Autobiography*, the critique of racism (and even its contradictions) falls under traditional patriarchal presumptions regarding self-determination, citizenship, and manhood.

Because Black people are positioned as witnesses to and symbols of each other's degradation, representations of intraracial conflicts over the reimagining of slavery and its legacies occupy a central role in the development of the Black radical tradition during the Black Power era and beyond. During the era of Black Power insurgency, reimagining the slave as rebellious was far more salient. Black women writers, however, refused to allow this narrative to go uninterrupted. They insisted on returning to the historical wound of sexual violence and the way it shaped intimate antagonisms and possibilities for racial justice. Black women writers also expressed their discontent over the traditional interpretation of slave history, particularly the silencing and erasure of their experiences that occur because of the patriarchal reimagining of the heroic rebel slave. Black women authors are actually a central voice in the neo-slave narrative genre, from Margaret Walker's *Jubilee* (1966) to Toni Morrison's *Beloved*

---

22. See Estes, *I Am a Man! Race, Manhood, and the Civil Rights Movement* (Chapel Hill: University of North Carolina Press, 2005), 8.

(1987). These authors' texts center the sexual violence, coercion, and instrumentalization of enslaved women that reinforced the system of chattel slavery. Such revisions of slavery emphasize racialized, sexual exploitation as an integral aspect, rather than a by-product, of New World slavery. Instead of a demand for racial and gendered recognition as seen within masculinist reinterpretations of slavery, Black women instantiate a "politics of refusal" through their insistence on registering the decisive injury of racialized sexual violence. Black women's vision of liberation would not permit them to align with a view of equality rooted in a traditional form of patriarchy—even in a moment of danger, of provisional victory, and of continued assault on Black people's position in U.S. politics and society. What they challenge is the view that creating a form of Black masculinity equal to White masculinity would be the cure to White supremacy.

How does a community, whether imaginatively or politically, contend with the legacy of rape and sexual violence? Acknowledging Black women's subjection to sexual violence as a form of racial terror is imperative to grappling with the exercise of racism and formulating strategies to subvert it. Nevertheless, an exclusive insistence on Black women's specific racial injury risks minimizing Black men's wounding around emasculation. While Black men and women can experience racism differently, addressing their unique grievances should not result in a zero-sum game over whose oppression is worse. Otherwise, we could wind up seeking the recognition of gender in the name of addressing race, insisting that Black women ignore their gender allegedly to help their race, but in fact by undermining the chance for racial emancipation too. The desire for gender "respectability," or for the recognition of patriarchal authority, offers Black women or men an entry into normativity that does not oppose the hegemonic frameworks for racial and gender recognition. Without recognizing that racial terror, whatever its form, operates to diminish the lives and worth of Black people collectively, we diminish the political implications of how Black men and women negotiate the imposition of nonnormativity by refusing an intersectional analysis of Black experience and subjectivity.[23]

---

23. On Blacks' negotiation of nonnormativity in popular culture, see Ferguson, *Aberrations in Black: Toward a Queer of Color Critique* (2004), and E. Patrick John-

In their refusal of Black women's experiences of racism and emphases on recuperating what Patricia Hill Collins[24] describes as "hegemonic masculinity," the dominant narratives of slavery and ongoing racial oppression threaten racial justice. This becomes especially clear in the wake of the Black insurgency that was taking place when Gayl Jones wrote her neo-slave narrative *Corregidora*. Published in 1975, *Corregidora* thematizes the struggles inherent in narrating and bearing witness to the trauma of slavery, and how these conflicts play out intraracially. The novel gives expression to the female ancestors' experiences of subjugation initially *seeming* to eschew Black male responses to the dominant representations of slavery. While the novel focuses on and gives space to the articulation of Black women's wound, the narrative seeks to understand a basis of resistance grounded in intraracial reconciliation within and across gendered positions.

The violence Mutt inflicts on his wife further symbolizes the threat to Black women's voice, precisely because the abuse she endures imperils her ability to sing publicly (creativity), her ability to provide testimony (evidence), and her sexual identity (claims to her body). In turn, Ursa's husband Mutt also bears evidence of the long history that shapes his name. The name *Mutt* signifies the denial or refusal of ancestry without legitimate or legitimating paternity. His "name" implies sexual transgression while simultaneously repudiating any legitimate claim to patriarchal authority. Mutt's wish to stop men from possessing Ursa with their gaze and her desire to assert her sexuality for a collective political project stage the confrontation between wounds, between competing desires for recognition of their racial and gendered subjectivities. The opening of *Corregidora* positions Black masculinist aspirations for patriarchal legitimacy and Black feminist insistence on their injury as a painful though necessary site of intimate antagonism.

Ursa Corregidora's healing process throughout the novel requires her to decide how the intergenerational agreement to provide evidence will be fulfilled and to develop the imagination that enables

---

son, *Appropriating Blackness: Performance and the Politics of Authenticity* (Durham; London: Duke University Press, 2003).

24. Patricia Hill Collins, *Black Sexual Politics: African Americans, Gender, and the New Racism* (New York: Routledge, 2004), 186.

such work. She probes the function of African American women's sexual violation in producing racial subjugation. Her analyses force her to "return" to the plantation to gain insight about her female ancestors' staging of "intimate refusal" and Black men's insistence on masculine recognition as competing forms of resistance. Intimate refusal in this context refers to Black women's radical reappropriation of their bodies and sexuality in order to register the injury of sexual violence that is otherwise so forcefully disavowed.

Sexual violence and the impossibility of Ursa's parenthood conjure what Hortense Spillers calls the "originating metaphors of captivity and mutilation"[25] used to distinguish and define the condition of the enslaved. In other words, slavery as a point of origin in the formation of the modern Black subject includes centrally the act and threat of sexual transgression in producing racial subordination. *Corregidora* portrays the inscription of patriarchal desire on Black women's bodies and psyches as well. The Corregidora women all bear the surname of the slave-owner. Along with this genealogical reference to slavery, the intergenerational transmission of the narrative of racist and incestuous violence bonds the women to that primary experience as well. A central scene from *Corregidora* illustrates the multilayered constructions of memory, narration, and gendered violence in Mama's and Great Gram's overlapping narration of rape and abuse. As Ursa listens to this oral history, Mama and Great Gram merge into one voice: "Mama kept talking until it wasn't her that was talking, but Great Gram" (124). The slave-owner Corregidora considered Great Gram his "gold pussy, his little golden piece," the property through which he amasses capital by selling "black" sexuality, and enslaving the offspring.

Corregidora forbids Great Gram from having contact with Black men, but finds her in conversation with a Black male who like Mutt

---

25. Hortense Spillers discusses how the sexual violation of enslaved Black women and their inability to claim their children situates the Black female outside of the traditional symbolics of female gender in "Mama's Baby, Papa's Maybe: An American Grammar Book" and in "'The Permanent Obliquity of an In(pha)llibly Straight'": In the Time of the Daughters and the Fathers." Both essays appear in *Black, White, and in Color: Essays on American Literature and Culture* (Chicago: University of Chicago Press, 2003), 228, 249.

is denied a "proper name." Having entrusted Great Gram with a secret, and later realizing that their meeting had been discovered, the man runs away pursued by mob and hounds. At this moment in the narrative the brutalization of this Black male and Great Gram's sexual abuse converge, for

> [Corregidora] was up there fucking me while they was out chasing *him* . . . Couldn't have been more than seventeen or eighteen. And he had this dream he told me about. That was all he wanted me for, was to tell me about this dream. . . . and then somehow I got it in my mind that each time he kept going down in me would be that boy's feets running. And then when he come, it meant they caught him. (127)

Great Gram's testimony refuses the construction of the "hypersexual black female" by returning the locus of sexual pathology to the slave owner and the system of racial domination. Her expression avows the violence done to Black women and their instrumentalization in producing subjugation. Great Gram's depiction also positions sexual violation as central to the historical revision of slavery, demonstrating how, as Saidiya Hartman describes, sexual violation encompasses rape *and* castration.[26] Great Gram's simultaneous narration of her rape and the boy's murder leaves evidence of slavery's evils against Black women and men.

Rape and castration are both instances of sexual violation "because enslaved men were no less vulnerable to the wanton abuses of their owners, . . . and because of the elusiveness or instability of gender in relation to the slave as property and the erotics of terror in the racist imaginary."[27] What Hartman calls "the elusiveness" or instability of racialized gender, however, is sustained by the erotics of terror within the context of racial domination and tyranny. Racial degradation, gender instability, and pathologized sexuality are pro-

---

26. Saidiya Hartman, *Scenes of Subjection: Terror, Slavery, and Self-Making in Nineteenth-Century America* (Oxford; New York: Oxford University Press, 1997), 80–81.

27. Ibid.

duced simultaneously and form part of the ideological reinforcing structure for making violence and disenfranchisement permissible.

Such dispossession also renders Black fatherhood, and the social and symbolic rights associated with it, an impossibility and a threat to the maintenance of the slave system. The unavailability of the terms *daughter, mother, son,* and/or *father* for the enslaved point to the role of what Orlando Patterson calls "natal alienation"[28] in determining the status of the enslaved. Reducing human bodies to property denied the right of lineage and institutionalized rape in the maintenance of slavery.

Black women's experience of sexual exploitation provides them with a unique lens in the analysis of the gender specificity of racial terror under slavery. Black men's experiences of violence, vulnerability, and dispossession shape their understanding of racial power and their visions of resistance as well. The dream the unnamed boy shares with Great Gram in *Corregidora* is his desire to run away to Palmares, a society of runaway slaves. His dream symbolizes his desire for freedom and recuperates Black men's historical emphasis on Black male insurgency. Great Gram recalls:

> He said he was going to join up with some black mens that had some dignity [. . .]. I said the white men had killed all of them off but he wouldn't believe me. He said that was what his big dream was, to go up there and join all these other black mens up there, and have him a woman, and then come back and get his woman and take her up there. . . . I said he couldn't know where he was going because Palmares was way back two hundred years ago, but he said Palmares was now. (127)

The boy's freedom dream of dignity, insurgency, and liberation is an appropriate response to the sanctioned terror and degradation of slavery. Yet his means for attaining this righteous dream of freedom is defunct, not only because his vision of Palmares belongs to the past, but because his concept of liberation involves making a Black

---

28. Orlando Patterson, *Slavery and Social Death: A Comparative Study* (Cambridge, MA: Harvard University Press, 1982), 5.

woman his possession, and considers her freedom secondary to his own. What remains "hidden" from his view while he pursues freedom is Corregidora's continued violation of Great Gram: "Don't let no black man fool with you, do you hear? I don't wont nothing black fucking with my pussy" (ibid.).

Looking to the past, to the history and representations of slavery, carries the potential of enabling alternative understanding about the intergenerational legacy of the expropriation of Black women's reproduction, of the denial of Black paternity, and of racial subjugation. Apart from centering Black women's experience of sexual violation and bondage, these feminist literary revisions of slavery attempt to take up Black men's subordination as integral to the processing of Black women's own. Rather than reifying Black men's emasculation, these narratives seek to posit a vision of liberation by bringing Black men's *and* women's experiences into view. *Corregidora*'s literary revision of slavery depicts the injuries that racial subjugation unleashes on Black men and women, as well as how these wounds can become invisible between them.

INTIMATE ANTAGONISM AND THE POLITICS OF REFUSAL AND RECOGNITION

> *Why did she have to look so whipped? She was a child—unburdened—why wasn't she happy? The clear statement of her misery was an accusation. He wanted to break her neck—but tenderly. . . . How dare she love him? Hadn't she any sense at all? What was he supposed to do about that? Return it? How? . . . What could his heavy arms and befuddled brain accomplish that would earn him his own respect, that would in turn allow him to accept her love?—Cholly Breedlove*
>
> —Toni Morrison, *The Bluest Eye*

As captured in the epigraph from Toni Morrison's *The Bluest Eye*, the inferiority, degradation, and abjection that emerge from the site of interracial violence complicate how Black people perceive and respond to each other. The legacies and exercise of racial oppression shape intimate antagonisms. How do Black men and women come to signify each other's subordination, and why does this conflict intensify beginning in the late 1960s? While the backlash of neoconservative policies, practices, and attitudes distinguishes the post–civil rights era, the "investment in whiteness" boasts a much longer history. As George Lipsitz reminds us, the economic, social, and symbolic assets gained by seeking, promoting, and sustaining White privilege provide incentives to uphold systemic disenfranchisement, discrimination, and denial.[29] Lipsitz's examination of White resistance to and refusal and renegotiation of fair housing policies and practices *throughout* the twentieth century points to an acute vulnerability in the logic of racial identity-formation: the domestic sphere. The threat to White supremacy that Black struggles for inclusion and equality posed was imagined as a menace to the White family. During and after the civil rights movement, this danger was made palpable through the production of the Black male as criminal. Under Jim Crow, collective anxieties about the potential loss of White political control and economic stability found expression in the representation of the Black male as rapist. The imagined defilement of White women by Black men represented fears of the White family's inability to reproduce itself and thus the impotence of White patriarchy. Lynching, and its reliance on kidnapping and castration, removed Black men from their families physically, and symbolized the definitive impossibility of Black fatherhood and Black patriarchy. Differing from the extralegal practice of lynching, residentially segregating and (or) incarcerating the now urban Black male criminal created lawful bases through which to preserve the spatial and symbolic division between Blacks and Whites in the post–civil rights era. As various scholars have shown,[30] many of the violent clashes between Blacks and Whites occurring during the late 1960s and 1970s were

---

29. Lipsitz, *The Possessive Investment in Whiteness*.
30. See for examples Lipsitz, *The Possessive Investment in Whiteness*; Thomas Sugrue, *The Origins of the Urban Crisis: Race and Inequality in Postwar Detroit* (1996); Arnold Hirsch and Raymond A. Mohl, *Urban Policy in Twentieth-Century America* (1993); Massey and Denton, *American Apartheid*; and Cayton and Drake, *Black Metropolis* (1945).

ignited by police brutality and (or) African American attempts to move into White neighborhoods.

The struggles over housing and residential space reveal an acute panic around defining and producing a racially pure domestic sphere and thus racially pure subjects. Although the domestic sphere is generally presumed to refer to the location of women's activities, influence, and confinement, it is important to remember that this realm is also circumscribed and controlled by male desire.[31] In a racist and patriarchal society, the domestic sphere can also be interpreted as a feature of masculinist power. For example, prosegregationists repeatedly appealed to the rhetoric of manhood and southern honor, expressing their struggle for power through traditional gender terms.[32] Convinced that "the door to the school room is the door to the bedroom," the White Citizens' Council justified a putatively loyal father's desire to protect his wife and children from the contamination that integration would unleash.[33] By anchoring manhood to citizenship, self-respect, and racial pride, these segregationists centered the recognition of traditional gender roles in the struggle for power. In other words, gender normativity would become an important benchmark in determining inclusion and distributing privilege.

The compulsion to protect White patriarchal power against the encroachment of a desirous rival casts Black men as errant sons. The representation of Black men as infantilized or dependent sons originates in post-Emancipation theories of Black inferiority but is reconstituted in the post–civil rights era. White male fantasies of the infantilized Black male or the Black Oedipal son displaced incestuous desire, the desire for the White mother, onto "blackness." This allowed White sons and fathers to disavow "incest" within the White nuclear family and their participation in incestuous violence against Black women. This disavowal necessitated protecting whiteness from

---

31. On the "domestic sphere," the "cult of true womanhood," and race, see Carby, *Reconstructing Womanhood*; Catherine Clinton, *The Plantation Mistress: Woman's World in the Old South* (New York: Pantheon, 1982); and Saidiya Hartman, *Scenes of Subjection*.
32. Estes, *I am a Man!*, 40.
33. Ibid., 45.

the threat to the nuclear family that the Black son poses.[34] Finally, the projection of sexual degeneracy through incest and miscegenation enabled the association between "cultural pathology" and the Black family. The argument for segregation and White supremacy, redeployed through the cultural pathology construction, gives birth to new justifications for structural inequality and de facto segregation in the post–civil rights era.

The presumption of sexual degeneracy underlies the impossibility of recognizing the Black male as "man" with the vested privileges that manhood bestows. Within the parameters of racial and patriarchal logic, Black male desire can never be legitimated. The violation of Black women becomes an exercise of White male authority and power. As Gerda Lerner argues, the rape of Black women also demonstrated Black males' lack of power, for they were symbolically castrated in their inability to defend Black women and lynched for associating with White women. Therefore, Black women were doubly instrumentalized as objects of forcible rape and as instruments in the degradation of Black men.[35] The sexual assault of Black women forms part of the reinforcing structure upholding a system of racial and economic exploitation.

How do the infantilization of Black men and the delegitimation of Black male desire interact with the exaggerated sexuality imposed discursively and physically on Black women? And, *how* do Black women become the targets of Black male aggression as a result of that humiliation? As stated earlier, the trope of incest in African American women's fiction narrates intraracial betrayal in the context of historical and structural oppression. I have also argued that the novels under discussion reveal the incident of incestuous violence prominently and focus extensively on the processing, significance, and effects of such abuse. Hence the "how" of Black women's intraracial violation, rather than the "why," leads us away from recapitulating arguments about Black cultural pathology and toward the more difficult work of thinking about how Black women writers grapple with the legacy of racial oppression.

---

34. See Heidi J. Nast, "Mapping the 'Unconscious': Racism and the Oedipal Family," *Annals of the Association of American Geographers* 90.2 (June 2000): 215–55.

35. Lerner, *Black Women in White America*, 140.

Accordingly, Toni Morrison's *The Bluest Eye* reveals from the outset the presumed secret of the novel: Cholly Breedlove's rape of his daughter Pecola. The novel was first published in 1970, appearing in the midst of public discourses and debates about Black feminism and Black Power. While Morrison's novel is not a neo-slave narrative, *The Bluest Eye* centers on incestuous violation, the desire for whiteness, and the struggles around affirmative intraracial recognition. Similar to his daughter Pecola, Cholly loved Blue. If God "was a nice old white man, with long white hair, flowing white beard, and little blue eyes," then Blue Jack was the devil and Cholly preferred him (134). Blue is an older man who, through his stories about Emancipation, fighting, lynchings, and women, captivates a young Cholly. Blue's self-sufficiency and presumed fearlessness become for Cholly a model of masculinity. In the absence of Cholly's own father, Blue represents patriarchal authority despite the perennial threat of physical violence and castration. Cholly Breedlove is Morrison's first example of the "free" man,[36] a fiercely independent, highly mobile, blues-like figure. The narrator characterizes Cholly as being dangerously free, for his life has already been riddled with violence, incarceration, disappointment, and dejection: "He was free to live his fantasies, and free even to die, the how and the when of which held no interest for him. In those days, Cholly was truly free. Abandoned in a junk heap by his mother, rejected for a crap game by his father, there was nothing more to lose" (161).

Yet Cholly is also socialized by his Aunt Jimmy, who raises him, and by the community of Black women who sustain them all. Because of the political, economic, and social structures of racism and sexism, these women are forced to take orders from everyone except each other and children. As domestic workers they run White people's homes; and "when white men beat their men, they cleaned

---

36. See Robert B. Stepto, "'Intimate Things in Place': A Conversation with Toni Morrison," in *Toni Morrison: Critical Perspectives Past and Present*, edited by Henry Louis Gates Jr. and Kwame Anthony Appiah (New York: Amistad, 1993). Morrison compares this figure to "what some people call the 'bad nigger.' Not in the sense of one who is carousing, but that adjective 'bad' meaning, you know, bad and good. This is a man who is stretching, you know, he's going all the way within his own mind and within whatever his outline might be. Now that's the tremendous possibility for masculinity among black men. And you see it a lot" (385–86).

up the blood and went home to receive abuse from the victim" (138). Throughout *The Bluest Eye,* Black women are precariously positioned as both objects of and witnesses to the abuses of racist oppression. Thus when Cholly's sexual initiation is interrupted by the flashlights and epithets from a group of White men, his partner Darlene becomes the receptacle for his humiliation, violation, and powerlessness. As the band of men violate Darlene *and* Cholly through his body, "he hated the one who had created the situation, the one who bore witness to his failure, his impotence" (151). While Cholly's "dangerous freedom" is created through abandonment, degradation, and objectification, it also demarcates the structures that render him powerless to protect Darlene. And while his form of freedom emphasizes rebellion and nonnormativity, it simultaneously disavows the lack of social, economic, and political power that collude in producing domination. This is not to discredit Black men's appropriation of an insurgent stance but to point out the disidentification with Black women's experiences that emerges as a central aspect of Cholly's dangerous freedom.

Several years later when Cholly sees his daughter Pecola washing dishes, "her small back hunched over the sink," and "her head to one side as though crouching from a permanent and *unrelieved* blow," the feelings of guilt and impotence rise powerfully within him (161; emphasis added). Pecola's posture reminds him in this instance of the many Black women who have cared for him. There is his wife and Pecola's mother, Pauline, who he meets while "she was hanging over a fence scratching herself with a broken foot" (160). There is Aunt Jimmy and the women of his childhood who often spoke of "the bruises they had collected from moving about the earth—harvesting, cleaning, hoisting, pitching, stooping, kneeling, picking—always with young ones underfoot" (138). And of course there is Darlene, with her head averted and hands "covering her face in the moon and lamplight. They looked like baby claws" (148). Cholly's rape of Pecola, his failed effort to "fuck her—tenderly," is a convoluted mélange of misguided revenge, misdirected compassion, and patriarchal protectiveness (162–63). The tragic outcome of his dangerous freedom and of the enactment of incestuous desire evokes the denials, losses, and confusion that define interracial struggles over the recognition of Black masculinity.

Nevertheless, the novel also suggests that grappling with Black women's experiences of violation and their unique position in the racial and gendered hierarchy can provide a basis for affirmative intraracial recognition rather than the projection of humiliation and degradation between Black men and women. Because Black women are forced to occupy the position of object of and witness to abuse, the "bluest eye" can also be interpreted as a blues perspective evoking the common experience of sexual violation (rape and castration) among Black people and seeking to develop collective consciousness.

Similarly, *Corregidora*'s primary narrative is not slavery's plantations but Ursa's recollection and processing of her relationship to Mutt from 1947 to 1969. Nevertheless, the principal plot development pivots around all of the characters' struggles to grapple with what can only be called a "public secret"—the history of racialized sexual violence and its legacies. "*You Corregidora's, ain't you? Ain't even took my name. You ain't my woman,*" Ursa recalls Mutt saying to her in one of her flashbacks (61). The memory of Mutt's words emerges from Ursa's recollections about what happened to Great Gram's male offspring. "I think they told me there was some boys," Mama confides to Ursa, "but Corregidora sold the boys off" (ibid.). Great Gram and Ursa are referred to as "my little gold piece" by the slave-owner Corregidora and by Ursa's ex-husband Mutt respectively (10, 60). Ursa's father Martin even calls Mama "Correy." The various names used to hail these women reassert their position as property and recall the originary scene of violation under slavery.

These names also align with the entrenched images of the hypersexual Black female that render Black sexuality abject, outside of culture, and thus unrecognizable. The specter of the slave-owner Corregidora is most strongly pronounced as the characters negotiate the terrain of intracommunal sexual intimacy, recognition and love. "*Dorita,*" "Correy," Jezebel, matriarch, are names that come from dominant mythologies about Black sexuality put in the service of disavowing Black women's violation. In the effort to buttress White patriarchy, these names also conjure the dispossession of Black fathers and the castration and disempowerment of Black men. The material, political, and cultural effects of racial oppression force Black women and men to be witnesses to *and* symbolic of each other's subordination. *Corregidora* illustrates that the avowal of Black women's violation also chafes at Black men's collective wound.

As Great Gram and Grandma discuss their experiences of rape, the histories of violence against enslaved Black men, and the importance of passing these narratives down, "what they didn't realize was they was telling Martin too" (129). Martin is Ursa Corregidora's father, Mama's first husband. Mama and Martin meet at the cafeteria where Martin works and Mama often eats lunch and dinner. Though Mama claims that she "wasn't out looking for no man," she remembers Great Gram's and Grandma's demand that she make generations. At the same time, Mama desires to be the object of Martin's gaze: "It was like I had to go there, had to go there and sit there and have him watch me like that" (112). Martin watches Mama in a way that implies a demand; his gaze signifies to her that he wants something from her. While Mama recognizes that this demand is most often sexual, she is ambivalent, stating, "Sometimes I think he wonted something else, and then sometimes I think that's all he wonted" (ibid.). This "something else" points to the hope and possibility for sexual expression beyond the terms of exploitation and possession used to confine Black women. While the couple never fully expresses *sexuality* together, Mama's recollections illustrate how an analysis of Black female desire must negotiate the historical legacy of sexual violence and intraracial forms of patriarchy. Mama's longing is entrapped between her female ancestors' injunction—to bear witness to the sexual violation of Black women and provide evidence—and Martin's desiring gaze. How can she possess her own body in order to bear witness, and submit to Martin as well?

Mama's choice is a compromise between the two demands. "It was like my whole body wanted you, Ursa," she explains to her daughter as she narrates the single sexual encounter she has with Martin (117). Mama, as her name implies, claims motherhood. Her identification as Mama, as mother, opposes the historic and symbolic degradation of Black motherhood. Nevertheless, her strategy of resistance and opposition refuses intimacy with Martin.

Great Gram brokers marriage between Mama and Martin, and he subsequently moves in to the house with the Corregidora women. In that home Martin overhears the narratives about incestuous rape under slavery and about the boy who dreamed of Palmares. Corregidora's control and possession of Black women's bodies, the way his exercise of ownership emasculates Black men physically and symbolically, and again the need to pass these stories down intergenerationally, are central themes in the narratives the women share. During the time Martin resides with the Corregidora women, Mama also refuses him sexually: "I kept telling him it was because they were in there that I wouldn't. But . . . even if they hadn't been" (130). Thus, when Grandma berates him for gazing through an open window at her naked breasts, Martin is forced to contend with his lack of authority and control over the Corregidora women. Martin becomes so provoked by Great Gram's and Grandma's continual "testifying" to their sexual abuse by the slave-owner Corregidora that he finally asks, "How much was hate for Corregidora and how much was love?" (131).[37]

Rather than avowing the women's narratives of sexual violence and abuse, however, Martin attempts to reassert patriarchal possession over Mama. When she later visits him after he leaves their marriage, Mama encounters Martin's anger and violence. After beating her, he rips her pants and sends her away from his home: "I wont you to go on down the street, lookin like a whore" (121). But why is this Martin's response? If he knows of the historical narratives about rape and violation, why does his awareness fail to produce understanding about the women's "wound," their desire for self-possession, and the impossibility of forgetting a violence inside the body?

---

37. Even critics of the novel falter in their attempts to interpret the triad between Black woman, slave-owner, and Black man, and often fault the women for their abuse. In these critics' reading of the intergenerational legacy of sexual violence, Black women are ultimately seen as co-conspirators in Black men's oppression and as responsible for their own abuse. Amy S. Gottfried writes that "familial memories distort [Ursa's] sense of self, and both of her husbands victimize her in part (but only in part) because she sees herself as a victim." "Angry Arts: Silence, Speech, and Song in Gayl Jones's *Corregidora*," *African American Review* 28.4 (1994): 564. Similarly, Richard Hardack argues that "the Corregidora women have become so socialized to expect violence, they seek men who will fulfill their expectations and on occasion even precipitate abuse when it fails to appear." "Making Generations and Bearing Witness: Violence and Orality in Gayl Jones's *Corregidora*," *Prospects* 24 (1999): 647.

The "mystery" that surrounds the Corregidora *women's* seemingly obsessive relationship to the plantation owner (rather than the basis of *his* tie to them) circumscribes intraracial possibilities for recognition, community, and intimacy throughout the novel. A significant factor of Ursa's physical and emotional process of recovery from the abuse and miscarriage is to apprehend better the complexity of the relationship between Corregidora's violence and her partner's behavior, between the historical racist violence against Black women and the intimate antagonism Black women continue to face. "*Always their memories, but never my own,*" Ursa recalls as she imagines what she would have liked to have given to her first husband, Mutt (100). Ursa remembers her childhood being filled by the stories of her Great Gram and Grandmama: "*My mother would work while my grandmother told me, then she'd come home and tell me. I'd go to school and come back and be told. When I was real little, Great Gram rocking me and talking*" (101). However, these are not the memories that Ursa longs to give to Mutt. What she wishes for is Mama's "*very own memory, not theirs, her very own real and terrible and lonely and dark memory. . . . Corregidora was easier than what she wouldn't tell me*" (101, 102). So although Mama carries "their" evidence, or fulfills Great Gram's demand for generations, it *seems* to Ursa that Mama "*wanted only the memory to keep for her own but not his fussy body, not the man himself*" (101). "How could she bear witness to what she'd never lived, and refuse me what she had lived?" (103).

Ursa's thoughts and Martin's violent reactions expose the entanglement between refusal and recognition in the realm of intimate antagonism and the sacrifice of intimacy that such an entanglement exacts. Black women's intimate, and seemingly infinite, refusal of Black men's demand for patriarchal recognition does not disavow Black men's injuries per se. Black women adopt a posture and attitude of refusal because they seek recognition for their unique wounds and degradations, for the pathologization of their roles as mothers, and for the denial of their evidence. The narratives of violence the women recount threaten to expose Martin's disempowerment within a system of racialized patriarchal domination. Black men's resistance of Black women's evidence is not a denial of their experiences of exploitation per se as much as it may be a safeguard against acknowledging the relationship between castration and sexual exploitation. The portrayal of intimate refusal and the demand for recognition recur as patterned iterations in the representation of intimate antagonisms in African American literature. Rather than a facile appeal to unity whereby gains are made at the expense of the other, the depiction of intimate antagonisms in *Corregidora* challenges readers to expose radical divisiveness in the process of redefining the meaning of resistance. The novel charges us with the task of developing collective consciousness about race, gender, and sexuality in our preparations to hold up evidence in the future.

One of the most important lessons that African American women writers and activists of the 1960s and 1970s taught us was the overwhelming significance of affirmative intraracial recognition to solidarity *and* to understanding the vicissitudes of racism. What I call "intimate cohesion" encompasses the activities of working through the collective trauma of racial subjugation, and positing forms of recognition that contain pleasure and political possibility. If, as Frantz Fanon and Hortense Spillers argue, the imposition of "blackness" is traumatic and renders one subject to physical, psychic, and discursive violence,[38] how do Black people develop the modalities of intersubjectivity they need for mobilizing collective consciousness in the service of racial justice? Black literature is an invaluable site for reimagining the past and envisioning a more just future. The anxieties about racial belonging, injury, intimacy, and recognition that the literature provokes can be productive openings that reveal how power works and how deeply social hierarchies become implanted inside of us. Because of the complexities that emerge in the struggles to gain empowering forms of legibility in a context of racial and gender inequity, I argue that intimate cohesion in African American literature is shaped by the historical legacies of racial oppression and the gendered specificity of racist forms. In turn, these constraining conditions are themselves also informed by Black people's efforts to redefine the terms through which they are made legible and to posit alternative modes for defining racial solidarity.

---

38. See Fanon, *Black Skin, White Masks,* and Spillers, "Mama's Baby, Papa's Maybe."

The intergenerational legacy of and continuing assault on Blacks collectively disallow for the simplistic and individualistic prescription to "let go" of the past and embrace or redefine one's desire. Rather, the reference to historical sexual violence in the formation of race and gender requires readers to pay attention to the structural dimensions that inform the complexity of Black sexuality and desire. The narratives of racialized sexual violation do not monumentalize that originary trauma but instead demand of their readers a historicized reading practice with a difference. Sexuality and race cannot be understood apart; one is the crucible for the other. As the various characters in *Corregidora* discover, more is required of them than simply hearing and transmitting the story of sexual violence. The obligation to bear witness is also about developing a consciousness about that narrative of violation that leads to healing, transformation, and justice.

Twenty-two years after Ursa Corregidora and her husband Mutt Thomas separate, they encounter each other again. Mutt asks whether Ursa remembers the story he told her about *his* great-grandfather. His paternal ancestor had worked as a blacksmith under slavery. Hiring himself out, he was able to purchase his and his wife's "freedom." After he was unable to relieve his debt from a group of unnamed men, "they came and took his wife. The courts judged that it was legal, because even if she was his wife, and fulfilled the duties of a wife, he had bought her, and so she was also his property, his slave" (151). Mutt's narrative reveals the entrapment of recognition in the context of racial domination and patriarchal authority. For the great-grandfather, the limited and economic possibilities for attaining something "akin to freedom" reduce family relations to commodity exchange. Yet it is the wife who is remanded into slavery; her body is debased and used to castrate Mutt's ancestor symbolically. For Ursa and Mutt, contending with their, and each other's, ancestors' narratives, provides an opening for *potential* reconciliation and intimate cohesion.

"What is it a woman can do to a man that make him hate her so bad he wont to kill her one minute and keep thinking about her and can't get her out of his mind the next?" Ursa wonders as she performs fellatio on Mutt and thinks about the succession of relationships from Great Gram and Corregidora to her and Mutt. Thus

Corregidora concludes in a manner similar to the way the Corregidora women's narrative begins: in the realm of sexual violation and the imposition to bear witness. This final exchange between Ursa and Mutt, however, represents a repetition, but with an important difference. Ursa's narrative, the text of *Corregidora*, compels her listeners to remember their own pasts, the consequences of that legacy, and the ways that racial and gendered violations have impacted the possibility for intimacy. In retelling these stories, in sharing experiences, we bear witness to the interlocking relationships between the wounding of Black men and the violation of Black women. Sharing these narratives of violation and betrayal is not without danger and complication, especially given Great Gram's warning about the denials of formal documentation ("they burned all the papers"), and Black feminist analysis of the overdetermination and pathologization of Black sexuality. Ursa does not reveal what she claims to "know" is the answer to her question. Gaining understanding from the ancestors' (and her and Mutt's) experiences in order to grapple with contemporary conflicts requires communion as well as radical acts of interpretation and translation. Such acts of interpretation or of reading are radical because, in the case of the Corregidora women, they seek to learn from the singular and "unverifiable"[39] of Black women's experiences. As the traditional channels for expressing grievances have been denied, the basis for affirmative recognition must be sought elsewhere and in a manner that avows the wounds and reverently leaves something unsaid. This is a call neither for more secrets and silencing, nor for further expropriation. Rather, affirmative recognition responds to an impulse of identification that creates bridges by working through the gender-specific historical wounds of sexualized racial violence. Such work enables us to posit powerful and transformative forms of recognition through the shared avowal of those wounds and impasses.

"I don't want a kind of woman that hurt you," Mutt asserts, to which Ursa replies, "then you don't want me" (185). In the conversation between Ursa and Mutt the couple must risk vulnerability to achieve intimacy. Although Ursa denies Mutt three times, her pos-

---

39. See Gayatri Spivak, "Righting Wrongs," *The South Atlantic Quarterly* 103.2–3 (Spring–Summer 2004): 523–81.

ture of guardedness also demands something of him. Deinvesting from traditional forms of masculinity rooted in patriarchal authority is a way for Mutt to recognize Ursa *not* as "a kind of woman that hurt you," "Black matriarch," "Jezebel," or as symbol of Black men's emasculation. Once Ursa finally admits "I don't want a kind of man that'll hurt me neither," the couple's embrace illustrates the yearning for connection across distance and a basis for affirmative recognition.

This interpretation of the novel's conclusion is provisional and a tactical response to a deeply entrenched problem, not an attempt at decoding a plot line capable of bringing narrative and ideological closure. The novel's ending attempts to state a transcendence of the binary between power and vulnerability read as weakness. Such "play" on the gendered and racial organizing logic of dominance and submission introduces a certain pleasure into the final scene wherein the movement beyond dominant paradigms also recognizes that they are within and around us.

The possibility for intimate cohesion requires grappling with the intergenerational legacy of racial violence, particularly the sexual violation of Black women as well as the limited perspectives of Black masculinity. Focus on the most vulnerable and on the production of vulnerabilities provides a point of entry for examining the complexities of intimate refusal and recognition and the potential power seemingly buried in intimate antagonism. How we take up the struggle for gendered and racial equality requires witnessing Black women's and men's testimony about the divisiveness of racism, and the development of community requires the ability to see "behind the veil" and beyond the "color line."

CHAPTER 4

What's Yours Is Mine

The Paradox of Intraracial "Bootstrap" Politics

> *Where my Color Purple? Where my god most high?*
> *Where my king? Where my black love? Where my*
> *man love? Woman love? Any kinda love? Why me?*
>
> —Sapphire, *Push*

CLAIREECE PRECIOUS JONES, the protagonist of Sapphire's controversial novel *Push*,[1] comes to literacy through her engagement with African American literature and politics, yet she continues to long for the intimate experience of intraracial love. Having endured the horrific sexual and physical violence that her mother and father wrought on her body, she learns, while attending an alternative school populated by working-class women of color, how to process her experience through her relation to her Black lesbian teacher Ms. Rain, the narratives of Alice Walker's *The Color Purple*, Harriet Tubman's radical leadership, and Nation of Islam leader Farrakhan's manifestoes for manhood and community control. Having moved into a halfway house, Precious remains committed to self-improvement: "I work all spring, memorizing letter sounds, writing in journal, reading books. I have read *Pat King's Family* 'bout white woman whose husband abuse 'n abandon her. I have read *Ain Nobodi Gon' Turn Me 'Round* 'bout civil rights. I ain' know black people in this

---

1. Cited parenthetically throughout.

country went through shit like that. But thas the deal here in cracker jack city as Farrakhan say. So anyway I made so much progress I won an award" (82). At the very least, the novel (and film) situates Precious's individual experience within a collective framework. This odd collection of leadership models brings together conceptions of Black female heroism, literary fictions of Black women's intraracial oppression, and fantasies of Black patriarchal community-building in a narrative about pushing forward and precious lives. How does one push forward given the experiences of ghastly abuse and intimate betrayal? How does one hold on to a sense of value despite the intimate, social, and political contexts that deny that dreamer the validation of her worth?

Precious is again devastated when she learns from her mother that her father has died from complications related to AIDS. This news, however, is exacerbated by her mother's homophobic and ill-informed comprehension about her own risk of exposure to HIV. Confronting her mother and her father's ghost, Precious does not encounter a proud history of Black feminine resilience, Black masculine leadership, or romantic literary closure ("Is this what I'm from?"). No clear direction for her and her children's futures appears. Instead she queries, "Where my *Color Purple?* Where my god most high? Where my king? Where my black love? Where my man love? Woman love? Any kinda love? Why me?" (87). Raising a series of questions about the functions of Black narrative, leadership, and community, the book also provokes its readers to ask what and where is Black love in the midst of a story about intimate antagonism in the post–civil rights era.

While attention to the novel *Push* and the film *Precious* emphasizes the depictions of urban poverty and intraracial incest, the pressing concern about Black politics, community, and love remain difficult to address. As with Morrison's *The Bluest Eye,* the graphic depictions of incest and Claireece's intraracial abuse obscures the novel's insistent engagement with the very question of what it means to love Black people, despite gender, sexuality, behavior, or class. The narrative seems to bring attention to the presumed plight of working-class Black people in ways that make them a receptacle for racial, cultural, and political anxieties that abdicate non-working-class

Blacks and others from connection to and responsibility for those very concerns. Claireece and her mother and father remain lumped together as the scapegoats for society's ills and, therefore, as symbols of social dangers and targets of social repression. They are presented as representative of the racial stereotypes that make them subject to or deserving of hardships they endure.

The novel locates the devastation of interpersonal violence across the domestic *and* public terrors frequented on the bodies of specifically workless and working class Black women in America's urban setting in the post-segregation era. The oppressive intrusion of welfare services into the lives of poor, vulnerable Black women references the context of President Clinton's 1996 welfare reform. The demand and desire to discipline so-called welfare queens existed long before Clinton's decisive legislation and even President Reagan's demonization of Black female welfare recipients. The Personal Responsibility and Work Opportunity Reconciliation Act (PRWORA) gained momentum and support from "tough on crime," "war on drugs" and anti-Affirmative Action discourses, organizing, and policies that identified working class, urban Black existence as necessary targets for reconstructing the United States.

Push was adapted as the film *Precious* in 2009 to international critical acclaim, including 2010 Academy Awards nominations for Best Motion Picture of the Year, Best Writing, Adapted Screenplay, and Best Achievement in Directing.[2] During her acceptance speech at the 2010 Academy Awards, actress Mo'Nique (who portrays Precious's mother) thanks "the Academy for showing that it can be about the performance and not the politics."[3] The film also received high-profile financing and production partially through Oprah Winfrey and Harpo Films. About the film, Winfrey celebrated "the power of great film, of great art" and "all the girls who are gonna see [Precious] and therefore be lifted up by seeing it. They're gonna [. . .] see that girl reading in a classroom who reads worse than they imagine themselves to, and they're gonna see 'I can do, I can do better. I can

---

2. Mo'Nique, since her Oscar win, has articulated her experience of being "blackballed" in Hollywood for refusing to play the game.

3. Mo'Nique, Academy Awards Acceptance Speech, 2010, http://aaspeechesdb.oscars.org/link/082-4/.

do better."[4] Yet the film raised *no* public dialogue about the shrinking welfare state or the demonization of poor Black mothers. In 2014, after the film's international success, and on the heels of global economic recession, President Obama signed legislation authorizing an over $8 billion cut to food stamp benefits.[5]

Push and *Precious* reveal the complicated terrain in which representations of intraracial conflict and intimate antagonism take place, especially in relation to putative intraracial class tension. Oprah Winfrey's hope that Black female viewers of the film would be inspired to believe that they can "do better" indicates the association between impoverished Black people (particularly Black women) and bad behavior. Could their presumed lack of motivation and self-esteem stemming from their cultural marginalization be ameliorated by their inclusion and valorization within the popular marketplace? Indeed, both Winfrey's and Mo'Nique's statements about the film imply their desires to shed any association between nonnormativity and blackness that the film and novel portray. Yet *Precious* and Mo'Nique's award-winning performance as Claireece's abusive and abused mother further solidify the separation between the respectability of the aspiring Black middle class and the stigmatization of the Black working class. Winfrey's desire for poor Black people to aspire to do better and Mo'Nique's gratitude for the presumed disentanglement of performance and politics project onto the Black working-class the obstacles to *Black* middle-class recognition. After all, didn't the film's endorsement by mainstream and celebrated African American media moguls do away with the presumed racism inherent in unsavory representations of Black suffering aimed at White majority audiences? If, as the logic goes, the Black middle-class establishment sponsors such a representation of Black working-class life and intraracial abuse, shouldn't we all take such a portrayal more seriously as an apt depiction of contemporary Black experience?

---

4. "Precious: Based on the Novel Push—Oprah Winfrey Interview," *YouTube*, November 9, 2009, http://www.youtube.com/watch?v=de_dggP-pHE.

5. Ned Resnikoff, "President Obama Signs $8.7 Billion Food Stamp Cut into Law," *MSNBC*, February 7, 2014, http://www.msnbc.com/msnbc/obama-signs-food-stamp-cut.

I have been arguing throughout this book that such depictions are not new but have been a part of the Black creative landscape since the 1920s. The presumption that class takes precedence over race finds opposition in the representation of intimate antagonisms in the present. The so-called Negro problem of the first half of the twentieth century is now remixed into the racially and gendered unmarked "underclass dilemma" of the twenty-first century. Post–civil rights African American literature refuses the presumed triumph of class over race. Instead, contemporary Black writers, even those associated with post-soul aestheticism like Andrea Lee, Trey Ellis, and Paul Beatty, continually depict the linked fates between middle- and working-class African Americans. This chapter addresses these concerns, arguing that class remains a creative proxy for the unfinished project of Reconstruction, New Negro, Black Left, civil rights, Black Power, and Black queer activism. Despite the long history of these Black radical interventions, the current era continues to question the complex relationship between race and economic oppression. Examining intimate antagonisms enables us to perceive the ongoing critique of economic mobility as an indicator of social and political progress. Given the long history of representations of the complexity of Black subjectivity, familial fragmentation, and intraracial conflict, economic advancement appears as a paltry sign of racial advancement. Instead, these intimate antagonisms reconceptualize the complex negotiation of racial community across class, through disappointment, and towards new images of Black life.

DOLLAR CONSCIOUSNESS: CLASS CONFLICT AND THE REPRESENTATION OF SUBORDINATION

A certain cognitive dissonance emerges that provokes the intimate antagonisms manifest in contemporary African American literature. Such dissonance again rewrites double consciousness intraracially and stages a conflict between the expectations of Black people's full participation and recognition within the United States and Black people's ongoing radical critique of the terms for inclusion. This critique exposes various unresolved concerns, including racial, economic, and gender subordination. Given that these axes of power were always at stake, the epistemological conflict that I describe encapsulates how Black people negotiate incarceration, welfare, and racial discrimination and segregation intraracially.

These issues, however, are subsumed under socioeconomic status and the notions of vulnerability and ability that accompany it. The American Dream has largely been understood in economic and racial terms. College education, professional employment, homeownership, and familial normativity are often markers of economic success and, if available to non-White people, they indicate the waning significance of race and racism. In the discussion and representation of subordination, such notions produce discourses that privilege and legitimate what are actually neoliberal forms of individualism. Jodi Melamed argues that with "the apotheosis of the individual in neoliberal rationality, it has become even easier for discourses to present themselves as essentially antiracist or multicultural even as they misattribute racialized social and economic dysfunction to the choices and personalities of individuals."[6] Neoliberal multiculturalism abstracts race issues and, in place of reference to race, it speaks to "difference" as a way of coding people for insertion into neoliberalism. Presumed deviance, criminality, and abject poverty root out poor Black people from inclusion and, in contrast, mark out the terms for those worthy of benefiting from neoliberal circuits of exchange and value. These dynamics reinvigorate and reformulate respectability politics for the contemporary era by substituting class for racial difference while exacerbating long-standing intraracial antagonisms. Public politics and popular culture converge to create new modes of valorization in the post–civil rights landscape no longer dependent upon explicit Jim Crow law and policy. Neo respectability norms align with neoliberal individualism that demands distancing from the thinly veiled terms of racial difference (through discourses of poverty, criminality, and domestic pathology). Intraracial bootstrap politics, at first glance, seem to reproduce dominant, neoliberal emphases on hard work, meritocracy, and good behav-

---

6. Jodi Melamed, *Represent and Destroy: Rationalizing Violence in the New Racial Capitalism* (Minneapolis: University of Minnesota Press, 2011), 140.

ior that make discussions about structural racism look like excuses for a lack of drive. Neoliberalism and expectations of post–civil rights class mobility can therefore masquerade as liberated racial consciousness.

Forays into the cultural marketplace to engage commodified representations of blackness become a way that consumption marks one's distance from poor Black people. In tune with the discourses that demonize Black people in poverty, Precious Jones herself disidentifies with the Black "crack addicts," branding them the ultimate stain on the race, that she encounters on her way to the alternative school. She is frightened away from the young Black men who threaten passersby, harass her, and menace the neighborhood. Because she receives welfare, she perceives her mother and herself as vampiric figures in society, both parasitic and invisibilized. Despite these negative representations of working-class Black men and women, she nonetheless seeks reprieve through an identification with the seductive, gyrating bodies of the Black women she views in popular culture and music videos. Commodified forms of blackness appropriate those same markers of difference but repackage them for circulation in the global marketplace. These forms paradoxically present Precious with another opportunity for valorization through the exchange circuits of popular culture, Black hypersexuality, and consumer capitalism. Her internalization of racist stereotypes, whether demonized or eroticized, complicate how we conceive of the imagined community that contemporary Black literature would create. In addition, her internalization indicates the absence of language available for representing an alternative presentation of those people-demonized populations. Claireece's process of coming to literacy thus parallels the reader's and viewer's need for new and counterhegemonic discourses about Black lives.

Neither the novel *Push* nor the film *Precious* provides a clear narrative of redemption for the Black working class, portrayed in these two media through the experience of a poor Black mother. Neither film nor novel produces a simplistic reading about proper motherhood, Black resistance, or universalist struggles against the odds, or even the U.S. opportunity structure despite race, gender, class, and HIV status. The refusal, or perhaps the impossibility, of narrative closure becomes a key feature of contemporary Black narratives about the obstacles of the post–civil rights era. Abuse, poverty, poor education, the welfare system, disability, HIV, trauma, and joblessness or limited employment are just a few of the impediments Precious confronts. The discourses that form public perceptions about these issues still take their cues from Moynihan's infamous report, blaming presumed single Black motherhood, Black cultural pathology, bad behavior, and ignorant choices for the struggles of the Black working class. Between *Push* and *Precious,* the eponymous fictional character collides with the text of herself.

Despite numerous depictions of intraracial violence (and even incest) *Push*'s urban emphasis on race, gender, poverty, welfare, and sexuality lend themselves to visual portrayals of contemporary Black urban life and struggle. One of the most important features of the novel that is lost in the cinematic version is the protagonist's narrative control. Distinct from Precious as focalizer of the film, Precious as literary narrator provides a conscious, and carefully guarded, presentation of herself:

> My name is Claireece Precious Jones. I don't know why I'm telling you that. Guess 'cause I don't know how far I'm gonna go with this story, or whether it's even a story or why I'm talkin'; whether I'm gonna start from the beginning or right from here or two weeks from now. . . . Sure you can do anything when you talking or writing, it's not like living when you can only do what you doing. (3)

Her process of coming to literacy thus reflects the development of her understanding of narrative control, of the power of narrative, and about what her voice, her story, can do. Literacy, then, is less about her learning how to read and write and more about how to confront and deconstruct the powerful narratives that shaped her life and identity. For example, in the first section of the novel, Precious relates her experience of being called to the principal's office and expelled from school. Despite the power that Mrs. Lichenstein, the principal, has over her life, Precious remains in control of the reported dialogue and shapes the reader's perspective of this authority figure.

I'm looking at her. I don't say nuffin'. Finally she say, "So Claireece, I see we're expecting a little visitor." But it's not like a question, she's telling me. I still don't say nuffin'. She staring at me, from behind her big wooden desk, she got white bitch hands folded together on top her desk.

"Claireece."

Everybody call me Precious. I got three names—Claireece Precious Jones. Only mutherfuckers I hate call me Claireece. (6)

The principal's knowledge of Precious is informed by the file on her desk that details her pregnancies, her age of sixteen, and her ongoing attendance of a junior high school. Such details, however, paint a picture of Precious that disables open dialogue between her and the principal. Precious remains silent during the exchange, yet her narrative control permits readers to learn of her repartee and anger against the principal's condescension. Precious's opposition to Mrs. Lichenstein exhibits both her attempt to master the narrative of her own life and the creative and social obstacles to doing so.

Consider, as well, what Precious does with the file the counselor, Ms. Weiss, has on her life. Having stolen the file from the counselor's filing cabinet, she rushes to her classmate Jermaine to peruse its contents: "I have just finished a session with Claireece Precious Jones. Precious, as she likes to be called, (I guess so bitch it's my name!) is an eighteen-year-old African American female. According to her teachers at Each One Teach One where she attends school she is a (I don't know what that word is!) p-h-e-n-m-e-m-a-l success" (118). The interjection of her reading practice and response maintains her narrative presence over the reading of the file as well as her opposition to its contents. "'She has a history of sexual abuse and is HIV positive.' ('She say she not put that in my file! Bitch!' 'If you told it to her it's in there. That's that bitch's job, to get the goods on you!' Jermaine say.) 'The client seems to view the social service system and its proponents as her enemies, and yet while she mentions independent living, seems to envision social services, AFDC, as taking care of her forever'" (120). Precious's theft and reading of her file presents an image of her stealing herself, of her attempts to confront the discursive constructions and confinements of impoverished Black mothers in order to challenge their hegemony.

As a poor Black mother on welfare, Claireece initially recognizes herself as representative of the devalued, expendable class. Both the novel *Push* and the film *Precious* raise critical questions about the text of blackness in its written and visual forms. Within the narrative, reading and literacy figure as prominent tropes for the process of developing language and, along with it, an augmented value of the self. References to and depictions of popular cultural representations and images of Black women's bodies as debased (violated) or desired (eroticized) also appear in the narrative's literary and cinematic adaptations.

Stylistic features like mixed media, parody, intertextual integration, and narrative irresolution and fragmentation recur in postmodern texts. Such stylistic emphases on fragmentation, hybridity, and multiplicity reflect and refract the destabilization of authoritative claims to truth and the presumed fixity of grand narratives, whether they are about the nation or the subject. Postmodernism brings the very question of representation into sharp focus.

What, then, about the Black postmodern? For scholar Nicole King, a postmodern critique, "which defamiliarizes received 'modern' identities," emerges with the questioning of a stable "black" identity in the post–civil rights era.[7] Black feminists, for example, were key in waging intraracial interrogations of difference. They challenged restrictive ideologies about racial identity, presumptions of heteropatriarchy, and consequent assumptions about political engagement and the basis upon which equality should be struggled for. Black postmodernism is also often understood (by scholars and creative writers) as a reaction to the absolutist aesthetic and political requirements set by Black cultural nationalism. A central and often-repeated critique of that cultural imaginary is its insistence on a narrow and essentialist construction of Black folk or racial community. As a result, as Madhu Dubey observes, "aspects of its racial politics calcified and began to feel repressive and untenable to the next

---

7. King, "'You Think Like You White': Questioning Race and Racial Community through the Lens of Middle-Class Desire(s)," *NOVEL: A Forum on Fiction* 35.2–3 (Spring–Summer 2002): 211.

generation of writers."[8] Contending with the shifts brought about by Black feminist, queer, and middle-class articulations points to the need for a more complex vision of Black subjectivity and community.

Considerations of the Black literary postmodern also take into account the interrelated set of significances between cultural production and the social, historical, and political contexts from which contemporary fiction emerges. The ongoing social, political, and economic crises that confront racialized communities in the present are central to what some scholars term the post–civil rights era. A principal goal of desegregation and the civil rights movement was to obtain the full recognition of Black humanity. Although legal discrimination was outlawed as a result of mass social movements for equality, the post–civil rights era has been characterized by policies that purport to be race-neutral but whose effects disproportionately risk African Americans' well-being. Policies and programs created to redress racial and gendered injustices have been refused, resisted, and renegotiated through entrenched representations of Black people as unworthy, undeserving, and, as Patricia Hill Collins states, unlovable. The effects of global economic restructuring, heightened economic exploitation, permanent unemployment, the disappearance of public spaces, increased militarization, and the commodification of everyday life have had an enormous impact on the conception of Black community and on Black lives. Thus, in a historical moment when we need to be attentive to the specificity of racial and gendered oppression, traditional postracial and postmodern discourses would argue for colorblindness and critique the fixity of race. Even still, the fixity of the Black signifier (as abject or Other) continues to legitimate the expendability of Black life, the erasure of Black public and autonomous spaces, and the insignificance of Black epistemologies as bases for reimagining social relations. Whether the dominant representation of blackness is circumscribed by phobia (Black criminal, inner-city youth, welfare mother) or philia (the Black athlete, musician, video honey), the complexities of Black humanity and Black

---

8. Madhu Dubey, *Signs and Cities: Black Literary Postmodernism* (Chicago: University of Chicago Press, 2003), 157.

experience are continually misrecognized despite official color-blind and antiracist discourses.

Therefore, traditional readings of the Black postmodern unwittingly reassert the primacy of the color line to Black cultural expression. The concept of a "color line" sought to account for racial segregation, a system of racial inequality based on the ideology of Black inferiority and the refusal to recognize Black humanity. In other words, traditional understandings of the Black postmodern remain anchored by the desire for White recognition, of an identity released from the binds of blackness. Madhu Dubey, in her analysis of urbanity and Black postmodernity, champions those contemporary African American authors like Colson Whitehead, Octavia Butler, Samuel R. Delany, Sapphire, and John Edgar Wideman, who, she says, "remain committed to imagining African-Americans as full 'citizen[s] of *the city to come*.'"[9] She goes on to conclude that these authors imply "that the book, the modern print tradition, will have to be refashioned before it can redeem its utopian promise."[10] In other words, Dubey holds out hopefulness for full inclusion, for recognition—seemingly modernist aspirations.

But on what terms, political or expressive, could Blacks be recognized as citizens? What are the terms of legibility that could account for Black humanity *but do not derive from Black ways of knowing*? The struggle within the Black postmodern, therefore, is also over the basis upon which such recognition of African American people, expressive culture, and political critique can be granted. The critical examination of contemporary African American literature and the postmodern exposes the quandary confronting the study of contemporary Black creative writing: what is the social function of Black literature?

For example, Colson Whitehead's novel *Apex Hides the Hurt*[11] (2006) also takes up the topics of community formation, representation, and writing in the so-called post–civil rights era. Ironically, the protagonist is an unnamed "nomenclature consultant" who has gained critical acclaim in his industry for the clever advertising cam-

---

9. Dubey, *Signs and Cities*, 241; emphasis added.
10. Ibid.
11. Cited parenthetically throughout.

paign to name a multicultural bandage Apex: "multicultural children skinned knees, revealing the blood beneath, the commonality of wound, they were all brothers now, and multicultural bandages were affixed to red boo-boos" (109). More than branding a product, the nomenclature consultant brings neoliberalism and multiculturalism together in the marketplace. After all, "what was a name and an ad hook if it didn't move the product? . . . The packages spoke for themselves. The people chose themselves and in that way perhaps he had named a mirror" (ibid.). Finding themselves in the language of advertising-commodified forms of diversity, these consumers form a new vision of community organized by its recognition as a market segment. The nomenclature consultant, a writer and creator of worlds, creates the people as mass consumers from whom he distances himself and makes a profit.

His reputation garners him the job of renaming the town Winthrop. During his research trip he learns the history of the place from the town's representatives, how it was settled by former slaves and given the name Freedom, how those slaves were double-crossed by the wealthy White Winthrop family who made their fortune in the barbed-wire business, and the new entrepreneur Lucky Aberdeen's bid to name the town New Prospera. With the desire to change the name from Winthrop, that family's claim over the spirit of the town has already waned. Albie Winthrop laments such passing: "my wife took it all" he moans, "took my name and then took everything else" (71). The past tense becomes his new roommate, for it is the temporality he prefers. The past refers to the greatness of his family name and their profiting from their investment in whiteness. In contrast, Lucky Aberdeen presents a vision of prosperity and multiculturalism and a change from Winthrop's era of segregation. "Everything around him was Lucky's appeal," the nomenclature consultant notes; "the inarguable common sense of Lucky's plans and blueprints—every minute since he arrived had been a rhetorical prop in some way. From a clinical nomenclature perspective, this was a no-brainer. These people were already living in New Prospera whether they know it or not" (174). Such a commodified version of multiculturalism also provides a position for the professional Black writer. In the novel his task would simply be to consent to the hegemony of

New Prospera and to affirm the community's new name. "New Prospera. New beginnings, blank slates. For all who came here. Including him," he considers as he ponders the possibility of the name. Even still, consenting to Lucky's neoliberal project brings about his own anxiety about his position as professional Black writer: "Was he supposed to honor the old ways because they were tried and true? Fuck all Winthrops, and let their spotted hands twist on their chests in agony. And forget the lovers of Freedom. Was he supposed to right historical wrongs? He was a consultant, for Christ's sake. He had no special powers" (177).

Freedom is the name the original settlers gave the town. For former slaves, the name is symbolic and indicative of collective aspiration. "Freedom. It made his brain hurt. Must have been a bitch to travel all that way only to realize that they forgot to pack the subtlety," the nomenclature consultant thinks sarcastically (76). For him, Freedom is painfully unimaginative. Regina Goode, the town's mayor and descendant of these Black settlers, reminds him of the history and presence of these Black families and their claims to space. Driving with Regina through Winthrop's Black neighborhood, the nomenclature consultant notices that the streets are named after members of the Goode family. "Everybody in my family is named after someone who came before. And if we didn't know them personally, we knew them as a place we traveled on," Regina informs him (127). She and her family instantiate a connection to the past that the nomenclature consultant, from his position as professional writer, does not share. Describing the Black settlers' naming of the streets and the town as having unique "marketing priorities," he wonders whether Hope, Liberty, and Freedom sound better than their experiences of racial terror and subjugation: "Better than naming the streets after what they knew before they came here. Take Kidnap to the end, make a left on Torture, and keep on 'til you get to Lynch" (128). But do the names change the character of the place, can they "cover up history?" (129).

"What is the name for that which is always beyond our grasp? What do you call *that which escapes*," he asks as he determines to find the term that would represent the town and the community anew. "What did a slave know that we didn't? To give your self a name is power," he concludes. With this statement the nomenclature consultant assumes a distinct role in relation to the community. Rather than imposing a name, his task is to accompany the community as they seek to name themselves. Learning the original name that the Black settlers offered, the consultant's decision is made: Struggle.

> Was Struggle the highest point of human achievement? No. But it was the point past which we could not progress, and a summit in that way. Exactly the anti-apex. . . . They will say: I was born in Struggle. I live in Struggle and come from Struggle. I work in Struggle. We crossed the border into Struggle. Before I came to Struggle. We found ourselves in Struggle. I will never leave Struggle. I will die in Struggle. (210–11)

Struggle, rather than an apex, integration, or even inclusion, informs the nomenclature consultant's approach to writing and meaning-making. The word *struggle* forces the confrontation with the complex and carried history of Black experiences, and it positions those who utter the term to bear witness to these embedded significations. Through writing, Whitehead's nomenclature consultant challenges the stability of the signifier in the context of neoliberal incorporation and the commodification of calcified images of blackness.

In the post–civil rights era, certain forms of Black cultural expression have achieved institutional inclusion and representation, especially jazz music and canonical Black fiction. Herman Gray, in his book *Cultural Moves,* discusses the recognition of jazz and African American trumpeter Wynton Marsalis by New York's cultural institution Lincoln Center. The African American writer Toni Morrison has achieved the highest form of institutional recognition through having been awarded the Nobel Prize for literature in 1993. Gray argues that such recognition by dominant institutions represents a shift in the historic pattern of exclusion and deformation of Black images.[12] Nevertheless, according to Gray, "the successful

---

12. Herman Gray, *Cultural Moves: African Americans and the Politics of Representation* (Berkeley: University of California Press, 2005), 15.

'occupation' of and use of institutional cultural spaces and the political claims that emanate from them complicate rather than simplify the very notion of black cultural politics."[13] Black cultural production becomes a site for political disputes over representation, meaning, and the valuation of blackness as a cultural expression. My previous discussion of Black postmodernity is illustrative of Gray's point.

The question of representation and recognition persists. One key area where this issue emerges is in the intimate antagonisms in Black literature depicting middle-class experience in the post–civil rights era. Even those who would occupy the space of Black middle-class status continue to delineate the connection between race and class. In this regard, class is not always a marker of economic marginalization but an indication of how race and class together shape the experiences of marginalization. In other words, Black and middle class together indicate the incomplete integration presumed by institutional recognition and class mobility.

Contemporary literature shares the complex encounter with the "book," or the textuality of civil inclusion indicated by Eurocentric notions of literacy. Just as Precious confronts the files and tests that portray her as parasitic, the novel *Push* endeavors to rewrite the text of blackness, to speak a truer word about Black life, and to maintain a connection to community in the process. Intimate antagonisms therefore take on the conflict associated with class conflict as they are depicted by the author's contradictory role in relation to the community she seeks to represent. Post–civil rights literature reveals a sentiment of what I describe as "burdened representation." Burdened representation distinguishes itself from the burden of representation that charged Black cultural producers to portray Black people in a positive light by describing the fraught task of creating a text of blackness that maintains revolutionary commitments to antiracism while simultaneously revealing the author's inability to do justice to that very task. The interplay between *Push* and *Precious* exposes how the realist portrayal of contemporary Black poverty life produces more disidentification with the urban poor than urgency regarding the ongoing connection between racism, poverty, and exploitation.

---

13. Ibid., 14.

The resulting capitulation to behavioralism exchanges the needed outrage against gendered racism for complacency within neoformations of respectability—self-congratulatory notions of achievement through color-blind conceptions of hard work and merit. Even still, current African American literature unveils the falsehood of such protective ideals, discounting less a blind faith in literacy and highlighting more intimate intraracial antagonisms between the author and the folk. In this way, these texts continue to engage the Black radical tradition by utilizing the contrariness of their texts and intraracial class antagonisms to challenge the institutionalization of Black literature and to point out the unfinished work of collective mobilization.

Post-soul, rather than post-race, becomes one way to characterize a new generation of Black artists detaching from the nostalgia for the civil rights era. Trey Ellis and Bertram Ashe describe respectively New Black and post-soul aesthetics that middle-class Black artists express in their irreverence for the civil rights movement's supposed sacred sounds and leadership.[14] While their analytic work seeks to create a critical space for middle-class Black subjectivities, creative expressions included in the category of post-soul continue to negotiate the conception of the book as well as the Black people that such a text would represent. Andrea Lee's 1984 novel *Sarah Phillips*,[15] for example, portrays the eponymous protagonist's flight away from the insular community of Philadelphia's Black elite. The first chapter presents Sarah in France, where she attempts to "cast off kin and convention in a foreign tongue" (4).

The novel centers the intimate antagonism erupting within the protagonist and between her and both Black middle- and working-class communities. In many obvious ways, Sarah Phillips, the novel and the character, contrasts directly with Claireece Precious Jones and the novel *Push*. Precious develops a greater sense of self and self-esteem through her reading of Black history and narratives of resistance. *Sarah Phillips,* however, is structured by the protagonist's flight

---

14. Trey Ellis, "The New Black Aesthetic," *Callaloo* 38 (Winter 1989): 233–43; and Bertram Ashe, "Theorizing the Post-Soul Aesthetic: An Introduction," *African American Review* 41.4 (Winter 2007): 609–23.

15. Cited parenthetically throughout.

from history and any connection to the civil rights movement. Both characters are compelled by intimate conflict in their familial lives, conflicts that seem to emerge from their respective racial and class positions.

Sarah's decision to commit her reflections to writing, however, is provoked by the story of a White American young woman whom the protagonist utilizes as the vehicle for her reflections on her own personal narrative. "During the wet autumn of 1974," the novel begins, "I heard a lot about another American girl who was living in Paris" (3). This girl, named Kate, hails from a wealthy Chicago family. She is a photographer whose rumored artistic and romantic intrigues become fodder for the gossip Sarah hears while living in France herself. From narratives about Kate, Sarah imagines her as "a kind of sister or alter ego, although she was white and I was black, and back in the States I'd undergone a rush of belated social fury at girls like Kate, whose complacent faces had surrounded me in prep school and college" (4). Sarah's encounter with the text of White females like Kate, especially as it conjures her memories of degradation despite her class status, inspires her own narrative.

It is from this realization of her dependency upon Kate's narrative that she expresses her pleasure at the French postal strike that facilitates her ability to "cut off communication with my family in Philadelphia, and I liked the idea of channels closing officially between America and France" (4). When her father, a Baptist preacher and former civil rights activist, passes away just before her commencement from Harvard University, Sarah's desire to discard Philadelphia grows "into a loathing of everything that made up my past" (ibid.). The patriarch's death simultaneously produces and fuels her *desire* for rootlessness, which for Sarah means detachment from the ties and traits that would fix her and her identity firmly within the Black community. Racial identity, especially as it relates to conceptions of Black people's radical history, features prominently in novels like this about the Black middle class:

> I had grown up in the hermetic world of the old-fashioned black bourgeoisie—a group largely unknown to other Americans, which carried on with cautious pomp for years in eastern cities and sub-

urbs, using its considerable funds to attempt poignant imitations of high society, acting with genuine gallantry in the struggle for civil rights, and finally producing a generation of children educated in newly integrated schools and impatient to escape the outworn rituals of their parents. (ibid.)

In many ways, it is the protagonist's desire for separation from kin and convention as a means to examine her individual identity that instantiates depictions of intimate antagonisms. In other words, she is unable to create a space for her narrative of Black middle-class experience without distancing herself from the representation of Black people collectively and her own experiences in relation to them. But even as she struggles to create this division between herself and the folk, she is forced to confront and thus negotiate the text of blackness.

Sarah emerges from the university "equipped with an unfocused snobbery, vague literary aspirations, and a lively appetite for white boys" (4). While in France she participates in a sexual affair with a group of three White men playing "a game called Galatea, in which I stood naked on a wooden box and turned slowly to have my body appraised and criticized" (7). In crossing the boundaries of interracial sexual taboos and restaging tropes of racist and gendered oppression, Sarah's initial attempts to separate from her racial past include the conscious performance of what Arlene Keizer[16] describes as "unruly desire." Keizer discusses "unruly desire" as a feature of Black women's narratives driven by scenes that reimagine the dynamics of pleasure in the context of subjugation (1668). Despite her desire for distance, engaging with the complex text of blackness continues to inform Sarah's narrative of flight.

"Sarah, *ma vieille,* you're certainly pretty enough, but why don't you put your hair up properly? Or cut it off? You have the look of a savage!" her lover Roger nastily remarks (10). "She *is* a savage," Henri adds, "a savage from the shores of the Mississippi!" (11). The boys' bonding over Sarah's abjection precipitates the end of her French

---

16. Arlene Keizer, "Gone Astray in the Flesh: Kara Walker, Black Women Writers, and African American Postmemory," *PMLA* 123.5 (October 2008): 1649–72.

fantasy, but Sarah states, "I wasn't upset by the racism of what Henri had said. Nasty remarks about race and class were part of our special brand of humor, just as they had been in wisecracking adolescent circles I had hung out with at school" (12). Sarah identifies her socialization in so-called integrated spaces that continue to be structured by White supremacist dominance. What the protagonist laments is the "hopeless presumption of trying to discard my portion of America" and thus the futility of trying to outrun race. While Sarah's experiences in France take form in interracial sexual encounters, they inaugurate the novel and the protagonist's reminiscences over her identity. Interracial sexual desire then emerges from her desire for racial detachment, and the failure of these relations points to the unfulfilled promises of mainstream civil rights emphasis on racial integration.

In the chapter "Servant Problems," Sarah recounts her time as a student at Prescott School for Girls, where "race and class were treated with energetic nonchalance" (53). When she arrives at the school in the mid-1960s, the autumnal colors of the leaves in the Northeast contrast greatly with *Life* magazine's "pictures showing flames blossoming from the storefronts in Newark and Washington" (ibid.). Again, Sarah compares her difficulty finding friends at school with the images of the civil rights movement: "A few years earlier I'd seen a picture of a southern black girl making her way into a school through a jeering crowd of white students" (54). Although Prescott invites Sarah to attend, "it shut me off socially with a set of almost imperceptible closures and polite rejections" (ibid.). It is in this context of civil rights agitation, her seeming distance from it and from middle-class mobility, that Sarah comes to recognize what the chapter refers to as servant problems.

"Don't you think it's rather romantic to be a Negro?" her White classmate Gretchen asks (55). "A few years ago, when Mama and Daddy used to talk to us about the Freedom Riders in the South, my sister Sarabeth and I spent the whole night up crying because we weren't Negroes," she adds (ibid.). The romanticization and tragedy her White counterparts associate with Black struggles contribute to Sarah's marginalization and her growing desire to fit in with the population of girls at Prescott. Yet in her experiences at and explorations of the school, she discovers that the democratic enthusiasm that Prescott and her classmates share does not interrupt the logic of the institution: "the teachers and students were white, and the domestic staff—a discreet, usually invisible crew of cooks, chambermaids, janitors, and gardeners—was black" (52–53). Although Sarah's presence upsets the school's operative logic, Prescott continues to find ways of making evident its racial hierarchy. Climbing the stairs beyond the classrooms and student residences, Sarah encounters the servant quarters. She is immediately shocked by three things:

> the deadly bleakness of the room; the fact that people lived on this floor; the fact that contiguous to the bright, prosperous outer life of the school was another existence, a dark image, which like the other world in a Grimm's tale, was only a few steps off the path of daily routine. I recognized the woman as one of the maids who cleaned the rooms of the boarding school students. . . . Another door opened and another black face looked out. . . . Thinking about the black people who worked at the school made me uncomfortable; I didn't know what to feel about them. (57)

Sarah's encounter with the servants' quarters and faces present to her a clear sense of recognition followed by an acute desire to disidentify with the Black working class. Hidden in the remote portions of Prescott, the servants indicate a truth about the school, its racial logic of White dominance, and the dependency on Black servility to exhibit the school's prosperity.

After this encounter, Sarah decides to audition for the school play *You Can't Take It with You*. After tryouts, she learns that she is cast in the role of Rheba: "Who was Rheba? . . . I leafed through the play and read aloud, '*(From the kitchen comes a colored maid named Rheba)*'" (58). Prescott manages to recast Sarah the student into the position of "colored" servant. Sarah's anxiety is that her class position may not protect her from racial interpellations. What's more compelling, however, is her resistance to being forced into recognition with the other servants. Servant problems refer to her thwarted attempts to separate from the Black working class as well as her irresistible identification with the serving class. Sarah is unable to look at the servants and not see herself. Finding herself in the narrative of Black working-class experience and representations (in the novel, at Prescott, and in the play) requires her to negotiate the meaning of her racial identity at the site of intimate, intraracial class antagonism.

Sarah repeatedly encounters and rejects established texts or representations of blackness for the narration of her life. Participation in the Black church, the Black family, Black female respectability, and mediated depictions of civil rights and Black Power struggles are all options for her to present a Black female masquerade. Instead, the novel presents a protagonist who first displays and then refuses readers' expectations for narratives recounting the emergence of Black womanhood or of the Black female bildungsroman. Such refusal is particularly salient in the intimate antagonisms that structure the novel. Towards the end of the novel she describes her romantic friendship with a Southern Black male student who photographs her while in college. Of the pictures, she states, they "were all horrible. After my first shriek I was able to observe, objectively, that while the body of the girl in the photographs looked relaxed and normal, her face was subtly distorted and her neck strained, as if an invisible halter were dragging her backward" (93). The novel itself challenges such mediated representations of Black women for their ability to define and fix them in time and space, or to drag them back to the most entrenched images of blackness. Upsetting the settled definitions and expectations about Black life, including Black mobility and aspirations, makes intimate antagonisms a theme *within* the novel and *for* the contemporary Black novel as well.

Readers of *Sarah Phillips* might presume that the novel "does not conform to their preconceived notions about black women's writing" (ix). In the foreword to the novel, Valerie Smith describes the contrary attitudes her students have toward the novel, despite the fact that the "circumstances of Sarah Phillip's life bear a striking resemblance to the experiences of many of the students with whom I have discussed the work" (x). Reading in elite universities in the post-integration era, Black students also grapple with the shifting meanings of resistance and accommodation in a space and time defined by sometimes more covert manifestations of racism. Her students desire that Sarah and *Sarah Phillips* exhibit "clear, decisive, and proud responses" to racism in line with the expectations produced by the reverence for civil rights and Black Power mobilizations (xi). However, the "shock of [intraracial] betrayal and recognition calls forth the less noble reactions of ambivalence, self-loathing, and denial" (ibid.). Representations of class division are the vehicle through which a series of intimate antagonisms are depicted. In this regard, class takes on a more complex guise than simply economic mobility, for cosmopolitanism, mobility, education, proximity to White power structures, and even the performance of distance from the Black working class, become facets of post-soul narratives like *Sarah Phillips*.

•

> All that you touch
> You Change.
> All that you Change
> Changes you.
> The only lasting truth
> Is Change.
>
> —OCTAVIA BUTLER,
> *PARABLE OF THE SOWER*

Octavia Butler's protagonist Lauren Olamina writes the verse quoted above in the journal that forms the narrative of *Parable of the Sower*[17] (3). By way of conclusion, I briefly mention these writings that create "The Books of the Living" and the content of a political philosophy that she calls "Earthseed." The novel is set in Los Angeles of 2024 in the aftermath and ongoing chaos of environmental and economic catastrophe. Textual materiality ("The Books of the Living"), regeneration ("Earthseed"), and intimate relations (touch) ground Lauren Olamina's philosophy in transformation and change. Intimate antagonisms between humans and the environment bring about ecological crisis and reflect the economic and social conflicts that structure the violent and exploitative relationships that characterize the representation of urban life in the novel. Intimate antagonisms, crises,

---

17. Cited parenthetically throughout.

touch, writing, and change point to the deep shifts in the structure of feeling animating African American literature in the post–civil rights era.

Parable of the Sower, like many other contemporary novels, reveals an epistemological conflict happening intraracially over what should have become possible after civil rights and Black Power struggles in comparison to what has come to pass. In the contexts of colorblindness and presumed racial integration, the persistent realities of racism persist. The ongoing production of economic and political subordination as well as the sexual iconography of Black pathology continue to deform dominant representations of blackness in order to justify racial inequalities and injustice. Representations of intimate antagonisms demand that we struggle with the text of blackness and that we struggle to create new language and new visions of liberation. The novels examined in this chapter still ask us to engage with intimate antagonisms in order to depict the many ways that U.S. society continues to be structured in dominance.

Yet Olamina's new book also provides an opportunity for a new community to find new words, "any words, memories, quotations, thoughts, songs" (327). As this chapter describes, the exchange of "touch" between Black people across difference contains the potential to change both. Intimate antagonisms emerging from the disappointments and frustrations with the backlash against civil rights gains still demand that we look to new ways of conceiving movement, progress, and community. Intimate antagonisms create an opportunity for debate over the meaning of love, struggle, and liberation. Burying the dead, remembering those lost, and planting oak trees, this community, like that of *Parable of the Sower,* commemorates life and moves forward with new language and imagination.

EPILOGUE

Intimate Antagonisms, the Undercommons, and the Town-Hall Meeting

THE SPACE of the university, higher education, and radical politics come together in new critical analyses of the struggle against domination. Stefano Harney and Fred Moten's seminal text *The Undercommons: Fugitive Planning and Black Study,* for example, looks beyond university teaching to the fugitive possibilities found not in respectable grade point averages but in "allowing subjectivity to be unlawfully overcome by others, a radical passion and passivity such that one becomes unfit for subjection, because one does not possess the kind of agency that can hold the regulatory forces of subjecthood" (28). Radical forms of intersubjectivity inform the pedagogical conceptions of the undercommons that the authors propose. Similarly, Robin Kelley's article "Black Study, Black Struggle" takes to the university campus in order to emphasize the struggle involved in love, study, and the opposition to oppression. Higher education, these scholars indicate, is not a site of refuge but one of challenging the racial status quo. Intimate antagonisms provide a unique forum for debating the obstacles to transformation and mobilizing against all that stands in the way of love and justice. During my second year of undergraduate study at UCLA, the Black Student Union (BSU) decided to host a forum entitled "Dissed by Your Own Kind" in order to do exactly that.

Confused and frustrated by the struggle to involve Black students in the organization's activities, members of the student union expropriated a large lecture hall to gather and to gauge the hurts and hang-ups that made Black students leery of BSU and of each other. The forum attracted a diverse array of Black students, athletes and activists, hip squares and hip-hop poets, biracial brothers and dark-skinned sisters, men and (many more) women. Only PAC-10 sporting events could possibly assemble such a diverse crowd. The lecture hall was tense as the moderator opened the meeting for discussion. Then, the room exploded.

Black women expressed their anger over their seeming invisibility to Black men who refused to acknowledge them when they were with their non-Black girlfriends. They found it hard to understand why Black intimate relationships were not prominent in BSU's attempts to gain members in the midst of LAPD's notorious brutality and racialized poverty in the city. Students articulated rage at the presumed arrogance of a Black women's sorority notorious for only accepting fair-skinned women. Greek letter-society members were forced to admit their prejudice; some even spoke of the struggle to sway the general mindset of their respective organizations and their pains at not being able to pledge with friends who didn't fit the color-conscious bill.

Low-income students' rage at living in the shadows of Bel Air, struggling to pay the ever-increasing costs of UCLA attendance, and often sharing financial aid monies with their families, was exacerbated by their feelings of alienation from other students who seemed to bear the economic burdens of higher education with ease. Working-class students' economic hardship reflected the unfinished efforts of civil rights and Black Power mobilizations and embarrassed Black students whose parents had financed their education and even bought them cars for school. Should they feel less Black because their parents could afford their academic studies and were models of Black success? Whispering to each, they wondered why Black people "keep each other down."

A Black lesbian emphasized her sexuality to demand an end to the sexual harassment she experienced from Black male students. "I don't want you," she stated with resolve before sitting back and allowing her tears to flow. Biracial students spoke about the frustration they felt from the constant pressure to identify themselves *exclusively* as African American, to assert their allegiance to progressive Black politics, and to relinquish any privilege resulting from skin color, hair texture, or parentage. Black athletes were among the most uncomfortable group in attendance. Black athletes were highly visible on campus and generally perceived as enjoying privileged status. As many of them came from low-income backgrounds, a few athletes explained how the sports program created tremendous dependence on the university for financial, academic, and subsistence support. This relationship of dependence rendered them vulnerable to extraordinary levels of university surveillance and supervision. In turn, this also produced isolation from other Black student programs, and resentment from other Black students who knew little about student athletes' experiences.

Although many of the statements made that night remain with me, there was one voice that I can never forget. Rebelling against the tears that threatened to choke her comments, a woman spoke of the pain she felt daily on campus. She was a first-generation, low-income student who, like many of us, struggled daily with seemingly indifferent professors, alienating curricula, and perspectives that dismissed or plainly ignored the presence and contributions of people of color. Apart from these and other factors that set up students and especially students of color to fail, her boiling point was reached by a dynamic she repeatedly endured with people in the lecture hall that night: their refusal to say "hello." In many ways, this student's comment encapsulated the varied expressions that the attendees and organizers of "Dissed by Your Own Kind" sought to address: the internal fracture of racial community and how they manifest in intimate antagonisms.

Six months after the forum, four days of "civil unrest" erupted all over Los Angeles's public spaces and commercial zones. The acquittal of four White police officers—among several other uniformed though "innocent" onlookers—who had been videotaped brutally beating motorist Rodney King was the catalyst for the rebellion. As with previous urban uprisings across the country, sanctioned police brutality ignited a long-smoldering fuse in response to virulent exercises of racism manifested in state violence, hostile policing, and the isolation of the inner city. During this moment of crisis, the public fight over control of LA's streets reveals an important dimension of the story about racial communities in the 1990s.

The forum at UCLA gave Black students the opportunity to consider their experiences of invisibility and alienation in light of cuts to financial aid and threats to affirmative action programs and their residence in a city bursting with racial tensions. As the arguments in favor of dismantling or reducing such programs reproduced discourses about "familial responsibility" and "handouts" and constructed students of color as undeserving, Black students' feelings of isolation reflected a different dimension of the same political and economic restructuring. During the 1990s, UCLA also became a hotbed of student activity, including protests against fee hikes and financial aid cuts that disproportionately impacted students of color; student canvassing against Propositions 187 and 209; and the 1993 hunger strike that resulted in the creation of the Cesar E. Chavez Center for Interdisciplinary Study. Varieties of "Dissed by Your Own Kind" have also become popular fora for many student organizations.

The UCLA students' meeting also illustrates how difficult intraracial intimacy is to constitute. Shared racial identity does not automatically lead to recognition. But it also provides a valuable example of the town-hall meeting in the undercommons carved out of spaces hostile to radical Black epistemologies and critique. Intimate antagonisms are crucial to the work that goes on in the negotiation of higher education and in developing radical reading practices. In this context, "Black Women Writers" was the course I desperately needed. I had been an English major and undergraduate for nearly three whole years, but this was my first experience in a seminar with an enrollment of exclusively Black women. Although many of the authors we read, like Nella Larsen, Zora Neale Hurston, Toni Morrison, Jamaica Kincaid, Alice Walker, and J. California Cooper, were familiar to me, our in-class conversations were not. The examination of Black women's writing provoked discussions about the importance of and obstacles to Black politics and organizing. No one was satisfied with Janie Crawford's relationship choices. Students spent a great deal of time questioning why Helga Crane was so invisible within her own community, and *The Bluest Eye* only compounded our own sense of the conflicts shattering the so-called Black community. Literary representations of colorism and class competition instigated considerations of the fractures to racial community in the 1990s. Instances of internalized racism, homophobia, and misogyny in the novels we read raised questions about the definition and function of Black literature in our turbulent times. We debated about whether the depictions of intraracial conflict enhanced our conceptions of racial community or challenged its very possibility. We wrote our essays on Black female empowerment and reluctantly moved on with our questions about intraracial conflict intact and unresolved.

The BSU's "Dissed by Your Own Kind" forum and the "Black Women Writers" course share several commonalities. First, both the forum and the seminar emerge from an underlying presumption of Black unity. Unity, the guiding narrative for Black politics and Black cultural analysis, provides the basis for registering the feeling of being "dissed" (disrespected or criticized) by other Black people, and for Black women's unique or intersectional perspectives. On the one hand, both instances of intraracial critique presume that racial community persists *despite* the articulation of internal division. On the other, both challenge and exhibit anxieties about the very basis on which community is defined and upheld. Students' responses during the forum and the seminar also reveal the striking absence of critical language that could interrogate intraracial conflict and imagine alternative visions of solidarity and/or communion. The open discussion of intraracial conflict on campus in the 1990s or in Hurston's novel from 1937 provoke questions about the long history of Black politics and organizing and how definitions of community shift over time to reflect the needs of those presumed to form part of that very community. Giving voice to those who have been silenced is neither more nor less important than cultivating a critical listening practice to receive those narratives and to create new modalities of connection. No one articulated the useful function of conflict, or the way cross-cutting issues would make the community stronger potentially, both in addressing wounds and in building more diverse and capacious notions of freedom.

The forum and the seminar also emphasize how intraracial conflicts are most often expressed and articulated in the realm of intimate relations, experiences, and interactions. Intimate betrayal intensifies in a context where unity in the face of racist oppression organizes and heightens the demand for community at any cost. Intimate, intraracial disappointments thus register powerfully and trouble commonplace definitions of community itself. Finally, the BSU forum and the seminar on Black women writers illustrate the significance of intraracial debate and dialogue that occur *beyond* the purview of the White gaze, in spaces that deprioritize White recognition and instead center the experiences, hurts, and knowledge that emerge from Black people's lives and conceptions of humanity.

Yet the forum and the seminar depart from this model in significant ways as well. The BSU's "Dissed by Your Own Kind" forum sought to address the intraracial conflicts that impede unity and thus political organizing. Dissension was the problem to be eradicated in order to produce political unity in the struggle against racism. In contrast, the seminar on Black women's fiction revealed intimate, intraracial conflict as a point of entry for thinking about the complexity of Black people's experiences and thus the multifaceted definition of community and possibilities for struggle.

This book began to take shape from my viewing of the late Rodney King's brutalization in March 1991. Nearly three decades later, we have been witness to too many more instances of state violence, terror, maiming, and murder of Black men, women, and children as well as the vile killings of Black queer and transgender human beings. The growth of the prison industrial complex, severe cuts to welfare, employment discrimination and joblessness, and rampant houselessness all characterize the development of the United States in the time since I completed my undergraduate studies. As James Baldwin wrote in the essay "Black English: A Dishonest Argument," the state of the United States today is indicative of its commitment to racism and of its refusal to recognize it:

> Not a thousand years ago, it was illegal to teach a slave to read. Not a thousand years ago, the Supreme Court decided that separate could not be equal. And today, as we sit here, no one is learning anything in this country. You see a nation which is the leader of the rest of the world, that had to pay the price of *that* ticket, and the price of *that* ticket is we're sitting in the most illiterate nation in the world. THE MOST ILLITERATE NATION IN THE WORLD. A monument to illiteracy. And if you doubt me, all you have to do is spend a day in Washington.[1]

These racist and racial realities continue to provoke new articulations and mobilizations of Black resistance.

The rallying cry and hashtag blacklivesmatter, for example, has been galvanizing and painful in its efforts to articulate the value of Black life. The protesters and protests remind us that Black lives have not mattered, especially when they have not been maimed, brutalized, tortured, and murdered outside of mainstream media attention. In the wake of media attention to police violence against Black people, conversation has inevitably shifted away from the national cause to local emphases on dealing with so-called community issues. And yet blacklivesmatter still calls for the affirmation of Black life. It provokes the question of intraracial conflict while distinguishing between state-based and intraracial violence. The movement has produced a need for attention to, analyses of, and new language for describing intraracial conflict.

Alicia Garza, Opal Tometi, and Patrisse Cullors, the queer Black women who founded the movement in the wake of the murder of Travon Martin, seek to "(re)build the Black liberation movement" beyond consideration of the extrajudicial killings of Black people. They also attempt to imagine and realize freedom dreams that grasp for more than a narrow focus on cis Black men or normative (respectable) Black people. In other words, this movement demonstrates intimate antagonisms within Black mobilizations against racial injustice in the context of a state that denies the systematic destruction of Black lives. The movement displays a politics of

---

1. Baldwin, *The Price of the Ticket*, 158.

refusal to go along with a program of opposition or of integration that disavows state violence, interpersonal violence, and intraracial hierarchies of value. Like the UCLA students, this movement understands that getting right within is central to transforming the world and imagining how to do so. Centering those that have been marginalized within Black liberation movements emerges as the opportunity for Black Lives Matter to elaborate a Black radical tradition in the present and develop new consciousness about the radical possibilities of reading intimate antagonisms.

How do we develop collective consciousness towards social justice? In the "Afterword" to *The Bluest Eye*, Morrison writes of the difficulty of structuring the novel:

> Beauty was not simply something to behold; it was something one could do. It was my effort to say something about that; to say something about why she had not, or possibly ever would have, the experience of what she possessed and also why she prayed for so radical an alteration.... The novel pecks away at the gaze that condemned her. The reclamation of racial beauty in the sixties stirred these thoughts, made me think about the necessity for the claim. (209–10)

Morrison points out the necessity of another gaze, an alternative perspective and epistemology on Black life and experience. Morrison's commentary on her fictional text and the radical activism from which that text emerges both seek to call into being an audience and a community capable of comprehending and reflecting Pecola's beauty. Despite, or perhaps because of, the narrative of intraracial abuse and exploitation, the "necessity for the claim" of Black beauty and of a Black community unified in its commitment to Black beauty and love compels Morrison's generative novel in an era of revolutionary activism and literary transformation.

Pecking "away at the gaze that condemned" Pecola, and by extension Darlene and Aunt Jimmy, requires exposing the hegemony of the White gaze on Black life *and* engaging another site of interpretation and analysis. "We were so beautiful when we stood astride her ugliness," Pecola's neighbor and sometime friend Claudia laments at the novel's conclusion. With Claudia, readers of the novel should also ask, how do we become witnesses to each others' subordination? Forgetting Pecola's experience of violence proves difficult because of its brutality—a brutality that almost makes us appear by comparison benign, honorable, virtuous, and justified in our respectable complacency. In later editions of the novel, beginning in the 1990s, Morrison laments how many readers responded to Pecola. Readers offered "pity" and "compassionate identification." "With very few exceptions, the initial publication of *The Bluest Eye* was like Pecola's life: dismissed, trivialized, misread" (216). But if the character was foil, antithesis, scapegoat, and the ugliness that made us beautiful, how could pity be anything other than manufactured sentimentalism, a demand for renewed commitments to respectability, or the refusal to engage with the significance of intraracial antagonisms? Claudia recognizes herself in relation to Pecola, certainly as foil (a symbol of their subordination) but also as community (the role of witness). Claudia understands that they are connected:

> We honed our egos on her, padded our characters with her frailty, and yawned in the fantasy of our strength.
>
> And fantasy it was, for we were not strong, only aggressive; we were not free, merely licensed; we were not compassionate, we were polite; not good, but well behaved....
>
> He [Cholly] at any rate, was the one who loved her enough to touch her, envelop her, give something of himself to her. But his touch was fatal, and the something he gave her filled the matrix of her agony with death. Love is never any better than the lover. (205–6)

The Bluest Eye is a communal narrative. The novel emphasizes the beauty and the pain of the most vulnerable members of the Black community, especially Pecola, but also Cholly. Without hierarchizing their suffering, the novel weaves together narratives of individualized humiliations and pains into a story of collective catharsis and consciousness. Claudia's comments express, rather than suppress, social memory. Her conclusion is a bold attempt to face up to what metaphorically killed Pecola and what is killing her community. Claudia's words illustrate the development of a collective consciousness about that shared oppression. Importantly, she sees how domination, in the forms of economic deprivation, racial segregation, shattered relationships, and daily humiliations, can also create divisions between Black men and women, across space, across class, within families, and between friends. Claudia also perceptively demonstrates that the remedies to these problems are not found in individualist solutions but in the creation of collective ones.

Perhaps this is the role that African American expressive culture has always played. How do you get people to pay attention to something they have no intention of addressing? The aesthetic of rupture, change, progression, and flow that characterizes so much of Black literary and cultural expression also lends itself to the examination of the representation of intraracial conflict as a necessary condition for the development of the Black radical tradition and, ultimately, to be better and therefore better lovers of Black people.

BIBLIOGRAPHY

Althusser, Louis and Ben Brewster. "Ideology and Ideological State Apparatuses: Notes Towards an Investigation." In *Lenin and Philosophy, and Other Essays*, edited by Ben Brewster. New York: Monthly Review Press, 1971. 127–88.

Ashe, Bertram. "Theorizing the Post-Soul Aesthetic: An Introduction." *African American Review* 41.4 (Winter 2007): 609–23.

Baker, Houston A. Jr. *Blues Ideology, and Afro-American Literature: A Vernacular Theory*. Chicago; London: University of Chicago Press, 1984.

Bakhtin, Mikhail. *The Dialogic Imagination*. Austin: University of Texas Press, 1981.

Baldwin, James. *The Cross of Redemption: Uncollected Writings*. New York: Vintage Books, 2010.

———. *Go Tell It on the Mountain*. New York: Dial Press, 1953.

———. "Many Thousands Gone." In *Collected Essays*. New York: Penguin Putnam, 1998.

———. "The Price of the Ticket." In *Collected Essays*. New York: Penguin Putnam, 1998.

———. "Black English: A Dishonest Argument." In *The Price of the Ticket*. New York: St. Martin's.

———. "Sonny's Blues." 1957. In *Going to Meet the Man*. New York: Dial Press, 1965.

Beal, Frances. "Double Jeopardy: To Be Black and Female." In *The Black Woman: An Anthology,* edited by Toni Cade Bambara. New York: Washington Square Press, 1970. 109–22.

Bell, Bernard. *The Afro American Novel and Its Tradition.* Amherst: University of Massachusetts Press, 1987.

Benjamin, Walter. "Theses on the Philosophy of History." In *Illuminations,* edited and introduced by Hannah Arendt. New York: Schocken Books, 1968. 253–64.

Berlant, Lauren. "Intimacy: A Special Issue." *Critical Inquiry* 24.2 (Winter 1998): 281–88.

Bonner, Marita. *The Purple Flower. The Crisis* (January 1928): 9–11, 28, 30.

Brooks, Gwendolyn. *Gwendolyn Brooks: Selected Poems.* New York: HarperPerennial, 1999.

———. *Maud Martha.* New York: Harper & Row, 1953.

Butler, Octavia. *Kindred.* Boston: Beacon, 1979.

———. *Parable of the Sower.* New York: Four Walls Eight Windows, 1993.

Carby, Hazel. *Reconstructing Womanhood: The Emergence of the Afro-American Woman Novelist.* New York; Oxford: Oxford University Press, 1987.

Cohen, Cathy. *The Boundaries of Blackness: AIDS and the Breakdown of Black Politics.* Chicago: University of Chicago Press, 1999.

———. "Deviance as Resistance: A New Research Agenda for the Study of Black Politics." *Du Bois Review* 1.1 (March 2004): 27–45.

———. "Punks, Bulldaggers, and Welfare Queens: The Radical Potential of Queer Politics?" *GLQ* 3 (1997): 437–65.

Crenshaw, Kimberle. "Demarginalizing the Intersection of Race and Sex: A Black Feminist Critique of Antidiscrimination Doctrine, Feminist Theory and Antiracist Politics." *The University of Chicago Legal Forum* 1989.1 (1989): 139–67.

Cullen, Countee. "The Shroud of Color." In *Countee Cullen: Collected Poems,* edited by Major Jackson. New York: Library of America, 2013.

Davis, Angela. *Abolition Democracy: Beyond Empire, Prisons, and Torture.* New York: Seven Stories, 2005.

———. *Blues Legacies and Black Feminism: Gertrude "Ma" Rainey, Bessie Smith, and Billie Holiday.* New York: Pantheon Books, 1998.

———. "Reflections on the Black Woman's Role in the Community of Slaves." In *The Angela Davis Reader,* edited by Joy James. Malden, MA: Blackwell, 1998. 111–28.

———. *Women, Race, and Class.* New York: Vintage Books, 1983.

Davis, Charles T. and Henry Louis Gates Jr., eds. *The Slave's Narrative.* Oxford; New York: Oxford University Press, 1985.

Drake, St. Clair and Horace Cayton. *Black Metropolis: A Study of Negro Life in a Northern City.* Chicago: University of Chicago Press, 1945.

Dubey, Madhu. "The Politics of Genre in *Beloved.*" *NOVEL: A Forum on Fiction* 32.2 (Spring 1999): 187–206.

———. *Signs and Cities: Black Literary Postmodernism.* Chicago: University of Chicago Press, 2003.

Du Bois, W. E. B. *The Souls of Black Folk.* 1903. Edited by Henry Louis Gates Jr. and Terri Hume Oliver. New York: Bantam Books, 1989.

Elkins, Stanley. *Slavery: A Problem in American Institutional and Intellectual Life.* Chicago: University of Chicago Press, 1976.

Ellis, Trey. *Platitudes: & the New Black Aesthetic.* Boston: Northeastern University Press, 2003.

———. "The New Black Aesthetic." *Callaloo* 38 (Winter 1989): 233–43.

Ellison, Ralph. *Invisible Man.* New York: Vintage, 1947.

Estes, Steve. *I am a Man! Race, Manhood, and the Civil Rights Movement.* Chapel Hill: University of North Carolina Press, 2005.

Fanon, Frantz. *Black Skin, White Masks.* 1952. New York: Grove, 1967.

Fauset, Jessie. *There Is Confusion.* 1924. New York: AMS, 1974.

Ferguson, Roderick. *Aberrations in Black: Toward a Queer of Color Critique.* Minneapolis: University of Minnesota Press, 2004.

Freud, Sigmund. *Beyond the Pleasure Principle.* New York: Norton, 1961.

Gaines, Ernest. *The Autobiography of Miss Jane Pittman.* New York: Dial, 1971.

Gaines, Kevin. *Uplifting the Race: Black Leadership, Politics, and Culture in the Twentieth Century.* Chapel Hill: University of North Carolina Press, 1996.

Gates, Henry Louis Jr., ed. *"Race," Writing, and Difference.* Chicago: University of Chicago Press, 1986.

———. *The Signifying Monkey: A Theory of African-American Literary Criticism.* New York; Oxford: Oxford University Press, 1988.

Gilmore, Ruth Wilson. "Fatal Couplings of Power and Difference: Notes on Racism and Geography." *Professional Geographer* 54.1 (2002): 15–24.

———. "Globalisation and U.S. Prison Growth: From Military Keynesianism to Post-Keynesian Militarism." *Race & Class* 40.2–3 (1999): 171–88.

———. *Golden Gulag: Prisons, Surplus, Crisis, and Opposition in Globalizing California.* Berkeley: University of California Press, 2007.

Gilroy, Paul. *The Black Atlantic: Modernity and Double-Consciousness.* Cambridge, MA: Harvard University Press, 1993.

Glissant, Edouard. *Caribbean Discourse.* Translated by J. Michael Dash. Charlottesville: University Press of Virginia, 1989.

Goldberg, Elizabeth Swanson. "Living the Legacy: Pain, Desire, and Narrative Time in Gayl Jones's *Corregidora.*" *Callaloo* 23.2 (2003): 446–72.

Gordon, Avery. *Ghostly Matters: Haunting and the Sociological Imagination.* Minneapolis: University of Minnesota Press, 1997.

Gottfried, Amy S. "Angry Arts: Silence, Speech, and Song in Gayl Jones's *Corregidora.*" *African American Review* 28.4 (1994): 559–70.

Gray, Herman. *Cultural Moves: African Americans and the Politics of Representation.* Berkeley: University of California Press, 2005.

Griffin, Farah Jasmine. "Textual Healing: Claiming Black Women's Bodies, the Erotic, and Resistance in Contemporary Novels of Slavery." *Callaloo* 19.2 (1996): 519–36.

———. *"Who Set You Flowin'?": The African-American Migration Narrative.* New York: Oxford University Press, 1995.

Hall, Stuart. *New Ethnicities.* In *Stuart Hall: Critical Dialogues in Cultural Studies,* edited by David Morley and Kuan-Hsing Chen. London and New York: Routledge, 1996. 441–49.

Hansberry, Lorraine. *A Raisin in the Sun.* 1958. New York: Vintage Books, 1995.

Hardack, Richard. "Making Generations and Bearing Witness: Violence and Orality in Gayl Jones's *Corregidora.*" *Prospects* 24 (1999): 645–61.

Harney, Stefano and Fred Moten. *The Undercommons: Fugitive Planning and Black Study.* New York: Minor Compositions, 2013.

Hartman, Saidiya. *Scenes of Subjection: Terror, Slavery, and Self-Making in Nineteenth-Century America.* New York: Oxford University Press, 1997.

Hegel, G. W. F. *Phenomenology of Spirit.* 1807. Translated by A. V. Miller. Oxford: Oxford University Press, 1977.

Hernton, Calvin C. *The Sexual Mountain and Black Women Writers: Adventures in Sex, Literature, and Real Life.* Garden City, NY: Doubleday, 1987.

Hill Collins, Patricia. *Black Feminist Thought: Knowledge, Consciousness, and the Politics of Empowerment.* 2nd ed. New York: Routledge, 2000.

———. *Black Sexual Politics: African Americans, Gender, and the New Racism.* New York: Routledge, 2004.

Himes, Chester. *If He Hollers Let Him Go.* New York: Thunder's Mouth, 1945.

———. *Lonely Crusade.* New York: Thunder's Mouth, 1947.

Hine, Darlene Clark. "'In the Kingdom of Culture': Black Women and the Intersection of Race, Gender, and Class." In *Lure and Loathing: Essays on Race, Identity, and the Ambivalence of Assimilation,* edited by Gerald Early. New York: Allen Lane; Penguin, 1993. 337–51.

Huggins, Nathan. *Harlem Renaissance.* New York: Oxford University Press, 1971.

Hull, Gloria T., Patricia Bell Scott, and Barbara Smith, eds. *All the Women Are White, All the Men Are Black, But Some of Us Are Brave: Black Women's Studies.* Old Westbury, NY: Feminist Press, 1982.

Hurston, Zora Neale. "The Characteristics of Negro Expression." 1934. In *The Sanctified Church.* New York: Marlowe, 1981.

———. *Their Eyes Were Watching God*. Philadelphia: Lippincott, 1937.

Iton, Richard. *In Search of the Black Fantastic: Politics and Popular Culture in the Post-Civil Rights Era*. Oxford; New York: Oxford University Press, 2008.

JanMohamed, Abdul. *The Death-Bound Subject: Richard Wright's Archaeology of Death*. Durham: Duke University Press, 2005.

Jenkins, Candace. *Private Lives, Proper Relations: Regulating Black Intimacy*. Minneapolis: University of Minnesota Press, 2007.

———. "Queering Black Patriarchy: The Salvific Wish and Masculine Possibility in Alice Walker's *The Color Purple*." *Modern Fiction Studies* 48 (Winter 2002): 969–1000.

Johnson, James Weldon. *The Book of American Negro Poetry*. New York: Harcourt Brace, 1922.

Jones, Gayl. *Corregidora*. Boston: Beacon, 1975.

Jones, Tayari. *Silver Sparrow: A Novel*. Chapel Hill, NC: Algonquin of Chapel Hill, 2011.

Keizer, Arlene. "Gone Astray in the Flesh: Kara Walker, Black Women Writers, and African American Postmemory." *PMLA* 123.5 (October 2008): 1649–72.

Kelley, Robin D. G. "Black Study, Black Struggle." *Boston Review: A Political and Literary Forum*, March 7, 2016. https://bostonreview.net/forum/robin-d-g-kelley-black-study-black-struggle.

———. *Freedom Dreams: The Black Radical Imagination*. Boston: Beacon, 2002.

———. *Race Rebels: Culture, Politics, and the Black Working Class*. New York: Free Press, 1994.

———. *Yo Mama's Dysfunktional: Fighting the Culture Wars in Urban America*. Boston: Beacon, 1997.

Kim, Claire Jean. *Bitter Fruit: The Politics of Black-Korean Conflict in New York City*. New Haven: Yale University Press, 2000.

King, Nicole. "'You Think Like You White': Questioning Race and Racial Community through the Lens of Middle-Class Desire(s)." *NOVEL: A Forum on Fiction* 35.2–3 (Spring–Summer 2002): 211–320.

Larsen, Nella. 1928. *Quicksand*. New Brunswick: Rutgers University Press, 1986.

Lee, Andrea. *Sarah Phillips*. Boston: Northeastern University Press, 1984.

Lee, James Kyung-Jin. *Urban Triage: Race and the Fictions of Multiculturalism*. Minneapolis: University of Minnesota Press, 2004.

Lee, Robert G. *Orientals: Asian Americans in Popular Culture*. Philadelphia: Temple University Press, 1999.

Lerner, Gerda. *Black Women in White America: A Documentary History*. 1972. New York: Pantheon Books, 1992.

Levine, Lawrence W. *Black Culture and Black Consciousness: Afro-American Folk Thought from Slavery to Freedom*. Oxford: Oxford University Press, 1977.

Lipsitz, George. *American Studies in a Moment of Danger.* Minneapolis: University of Minnesota Press, 2001.

———. *Dangerous Crossroads: Popular Music, Postmodernism, and the Poetics of Place.* London: Verso, 1994.

———. *Footsteps in the Dark: The Hidden Histories of Popular Music.* Minneapolis: University of Minnesota Press, 2007.

———. *How Racism Takes Place.* Philadelphia: Temple University Press, 2011.

———. *The Possessive Investment in Whiteness: How White People Profit from Identity Politics.* Philadelphia: Temple University Press, 1998.

Locke, Alain. 1925. *The New Negro.* New York: Simon & Schuster, 1997.

Lorde, Audre. *Sister Outsider: Essays and Speeches.* Trumansburg, NY: Crossing Press, 1984.

Mackey, Nathaniel. "Other: From Noun to Verb." In *Jazz among the Discourses,* edited by Krin Gabbard. Durham: Duke University Press, 1995. 76–99.

Major, Clarence, ed. *The New Black Poetry.* New York: International Publishers, 1969.

Marks, Carole. *Farewell—We're Good and Gone: The Great Black Migration.* Bloomington: Indiana University Press, 1989.

McDowell, Deborah E. "Introduction" to *Quicksand; and, Passing.* New Brunswick, NJ: Rutgers University Press, 1986.

———. "Reading Family Matters." In *Changing Our Own Words: Essays on Criticism Theory, and Writing by Black Women,* edited by Cheryl Wall. New Brunswick: Rutgers University Press, 1989. 75–97.

Melamed, Jodi. *Represent and Destroy: Rationalizing Violence in the New Racial Capitalism.* Minneapolis: University of Minnesota Press, 2011.

Mitchell, Koritha. *Living with Lynching: African American Lynching Plays, Performance, and Citizenship, 1890–1930.* Urbana: University of Illinois Press, 2011.

Morrison, Toni. *Beloved.* New York: Knopf, 1987.

———. *The Bluest Eye.* 1970. New York: Knopf, 1993.

———. *Jazz.* New York: Plume, 1992.

———. *Playing in the Dark: Whiteness and the Literary Imagination.* New York: Vintage Books, 1992.

———. *Sula.* New York: Knopf, 1974.

Moten, Fred. *In the Break: The Aesthetics of the Black Radical Tradition.* University of Minnesota Press: Minneapolis, 2003.

Moynihan, Daniel Patrick and the U.S. Department of Labor. *The Negro Family: The Case for National Action.* Washington, DC: USGPO, 1965.

Mullen, Bill V. and James Smethurst, eds. *Left of the Color Line: Race, Radicalism, and Twentieth-Century Literature of the United States.* Chapel Hill: University of North Carolina Press, 2003.

Otten, Terry. "Horrific Love in Toni Morrison's Fiction." *Modern Fiction Studies* 39 (1993): 651–67.

Pate, Alexs D. Foreword to *The Cotillion, or, One Good Bull Is Half the Herd*. By John Oliver Killen. Minneapolis: Coffee House, 2002. ix–xxi.

Patterson, Orlando. *Slavery and Social Death: A Comparative Study*. Cambridge, MA: Harvard University Press, 1982.

Peach, Linden. *Toni Morrison*. London: Macmillan, 1995.

Petry, Ann. "Like a Winding Sheet." 1945. In *The Norton Anthology of African American Literature*, edited by Henry Louis Gates and Nellie Y. McKay. 2nd ed. New York: Norton, 2004.

Randall, Alice. *Rebel Yell: A Novel*. New York: Bloomsbury, 2009.

Rawick, George. *From Sunup to Sundown: The Making of the Black Community*. Westport, CT: Greenwood, 1972.

Robinson, Cedric. *Black Marxism: The Making of the Black Radical Tradition*. Chapel Hill; London: University of North Carolina Press, 2005.

———. *Black Movements in America*. New York: Routledge, 1997.

Rose, Tricia. *Black Noise: Rap Music and Black Culture in Contemporary America*. Hanover, NH: Wesleyan University Press, 1994.

———. "Hansberry's *A Raisin in the Sun* and the 'Illegible' Politics of (Inter)personal Justice." *Kalfou* 1.1 (2014): 27–60.

———. *Longing to Tell: Black Women Talk about Sexuality and Intimacy*. New York: Farrar Strauss, and Giroux, 2003.

———. "A Symposium on Popular Culture and Political Correctness." *Social Text* 36 (Autumn 1993): 1–39.

Rushdy, Ashraf. *Neo-Slave Narratives: Studies in the Social Logic of a Literary Form*. New York: Oxford University Press, 1997.

Sandoval, Chela. *Methodology of the Oppressed*. Minneapolis: University of Minnesota Press, 2000.

Sapphire. *Push: A Novel*. New York: Knopf, 1996.

Simon, Bruce. "Traumatic Repetition in Gayl Jones's *Corregidora*." In *Race Consciousness: African American Studies for the New Century*, edited by Judith Jackson Fossett and Jeffrey A. Tucker. New York: New York University Press, 1997. 93–112.

Singh, Nikil Pal. *Black Is a Country: Race and the Unfinished Struggle for Democracy*. Cambridge, MA: Harvard University Press, 2004.

Smethurst, James. *The New Red Negro: The Literary Left and African American Poetry, 1930—1946*. New York: Oxford University Press, 1999.

Spaulding, Timothy A. *Re-Forming the Past: History, the Fantastic, and the Postmodern Slave Narrative*. Columbus: The Ohio State University Press, 2005.

Spillers, Hortense. "'All the Things You Could Be by Now, If Sigmund Freud's Wife Was Your Mother': Psychoanalysis and Race." 1996. In Spillers, *Black, White, and in Color*, 376–427.

———. *Black, White, and in Color: Essays on American Literature and Culture.* Chicago: University of Chicago Press, 2003.

———. "The Crisis of the Negro Intellectual." *boundary 2* 21.3 (Fall 1994): 65–116.

———. "A Hateful Passion, a Lost Love: Three Women's Fiction." 1983. In Spillers, *Black, White, and in Color*, 93–118.

———. "Interstices: A Small Drama of Words." 1984. In Spillers, *Black, White, and in Color*, 152–75.

———. "Mama's Baby, Papa's Maybe: An American Grammar Book." 1987. In Spillers, *Black, White, and in Color*, 203–29.

———. "'The Permanent Obliquity of an In(pha)llibly Straight': In the Time of the Daughters and the Fathers." 1989. In Spillers, *Black, White, and in Color*, 230–50.

Spivak, Gayatri. "Righting Wrongs." *The South Atlantic Quarterly* 103.2–3 (Spring-Summer 2004): 523–81.

Springer, Kimberly. *Living for the Revolution: Black Feminist Organizations, 1968–1980.* Durham: Duke University Press, 2005.

Stewart, Kathleen. *A Space on the Side of the Road: Cultural Poetics in an Other America.* Princeton: Princeton University Press, 1996.

Tate, Claudia. *Domestic Allegories of Political Desire: The Black Heroine's Text at the Turn of the Century.* New York: Oxford University Press, 1992.

———. *Psychoanalysis and Black Novels: Desire and the Protocols of Race.* New York: Oxford University Press, 1998.

Thurman, Wallace. *The Blacker the Berry.* 1929. New York: Arno, 1969.

Walker, Margaret. *Jubilee.* Boston: Mariner, 1966.

Wall, Cheryl, ed. *Changing Our Own Words: Essays on Criticism Theory, and Writing by Black Women.* New Brunswick, NJ: Rutgers University Press, 1989.

Wallace, Michele. *Invisibility Blues: From Pop to Theory.* London: Verso, 1990.

Wells, Ida B. *Crusade for Justice: The Autobiography of Ida B. Wells.* Chicago: University of Chicago Press, 1970.

West, Cornel. *Race Matters.* Boston: Beacon, 1993.

White, Deborah Gray. *Ar'nt' I a Woman? Female Slaves in the Plantation South.* New York: Norton, 1985.

White, Frances E. *Dark Continent of Our Bodies: Black Feminism and the Politics of Respectability.* Philadelphia: Temple University Press, 2001.

White, Hayden. "The Fictions of Factual Representation." In *Tropics of Discourse: Essays in Cultural Criticism.* Baltimore: Johns Hopkins University Press, 1978.

———. "Narrativity in the Representation of Reality." In *The Content of the Form: Narrative Discourse and Historical Representation*. Baltimore: Johns Hopkins University Press, 1987.

Whitehead, Colson. *Apex Hides the Hurt*. New York: Doubleday, 2006.

Williams, Linda Faye. *The Constraint of Race: Legacies of White Skin Privilege in America*. University Park: Pennsylvania State University Press, 2003.

Williams, Patricia J. *Seeing a Color-Blind Future: The Paradox of Race*. New York: Noonday, 1998.

Williams, Raymond. *Marxism and Literature*. Oxford: Oxford University Press, 1977.

Woods, Clyde. *Development Arrested: The Blues and Plantation Power in the Mississippi Delta*. London; New York: Verso, 1998.

Wright, Richard. *Black Boy (American Hunger): A Record of Childhood and Youth*. New York: Harper, 1945.

———. *Native Son*. New York: Harper, 1940.

INDEX

abandonment, 8, 46, 57, 87, 108
achievement, 28, 45, 119, 131, 133
activism, 48, 56, 57, 77, 78, 92, 148; interventions by, 121; respectability politics of, 6
aesthetics, 14, 18, 24, 48, 126
Afro-American Novel and Its Tradition, The (Bell), 95
Alice, 59, 64; Bob and, 58, 61, 63; Stella and, 62–63
Althusser, Louis, 14
antiracism, 25, 122, 128, 132
Apex Hides the Hurt (Whitehead), 128–29
Ashe, Bertram, 133
assimilation, 5, 13, 24, 62, 71, 74, 80
Autobiography of Miss Jane Pittman, The (Gaines), 96, 97

Baker, Ella, 10

Baldwin, James, 16, 17, 22, 23, 73–74, 79, 146; Black intersubjectivity and, 77; intimate antagonism and, 78; racism and, 76
Bea, Frances: double jeopardy and, 67
Beatty, Paul, 24, 121
Bell, Bernard, 69, 95–96
Beloved (Morrison), 97–98
Benjamin, Walter, 91
betrayal, 8, 46, 63, 86, 92, 95, 106, 115, 118, 139, 146
Black Boy (Wright), 58, 70, 71, 72, 73
Black community, 46, 48, 58, 71, 134, 148; conception of, 42, 51–52, 127; racialized/gendered violence within, 34
Black culture, 18, 53, 65, 131; degeneracy of, 94; exoticization/marginalization of, 45; production of, 66
"Black English: A Dishonest Argument" (Baldwin), 146

162 • INDEX

Black family, 78, 138; cultural pathology and, 106; intimate antagonisms and, 81

Black feminism, 21, 23, 24, 107, 115, 216

Black humanity, 12, 127, 128, 146; denying, 14; evolution of, 4; full recognition of, 127; radical representation of, 57

Black life, 45, 70, 72, 127, 148; counter-hegemonic discourses about, 123; destruction of, 25, 147; intimate quarters of, 19, 47; intraracial dynamics of, 29; levels of consciousness of, 80; portrayals of, 47, 73; rural vision of, 35

Black literature, 4, 11, 13, 20, 54, 57–58, 65, 66, 117, 123, 128, 133, 140; approach to, 16; definition/function of, 145; expressiveness of, 21; intraracial conflict in, 7, 9; language/ meaning/subjectivity of, 15; life-affirming possibilities of, 12; post-civil rights, 24, 121; reciprocal recrimination in, 9; social function of, 128

Black Lives Matter, 25, 147, 148

Black masculinity, 32, 49, 86; recognition of, 108; White masculinity and, 98

Black men: Black women and, 85, 91–92; degradation of, 105, 106, 109; dependency of, 93; emasculation of, 38, 67, 98, 103, 111; leadership of, 118; limitations of, 116; non-Black girlfriends and, 142; patriarchy and, 86, 112; political/racial justice and, 23; powerlessness of, 89, 106; representation of, 105; slavery and, 101; violence and, 102; wounding of, 110, 115

Black Metropolis: A Study of Negro Life in a Northern City (Drake and Cayton), 55, 56, 57

Black middle class, 46, 120, 132, 134, 135

Black people: common destiny of, 9; freedom dreams of, 147; language and, 17; misrecognition of, 15; police violence against, 147; progress of, 9, 61; racial history of, 89; radical history of, 134; representing, 72–73; as witnesses, 2

Black Power, 21, 87, 92, 94, 95, 97, 107, 121, 138, 140, 142; Black women and, 24; discourses, 23; mobilization, 139; New Left and, 96

Black queer/transgender persons, 10, 146

Black radicalism, 7, 48, 54, 57, 66, 73, 97, 141, 148; methodology of, 12; struggle of, 16–17; undermined, 10–11

Black Student Union (BSU), 142–44, 145, 146

"Black Study, Black Struggle" (Kelley), 141

Black subjectivity, 15, 16, 17, 18, 21, 22, 56, 57, 61, 62, 64, 73, 74, 77, 78, 86, 98, 121, 127, 133, 141; contemplating, 78; depictions of, 58; formation of, 65

Black women, 23, 88–89, 138; anger of, 142; Black men and, 85, 91–92; community and, 3; degradation of, 87, 109; gender and, 98; hypersexual, 101, 109; images of, 126; intimate antagonism and, 112; intraracial violation of, 106; meaning/knowledge and, 89; narratives of, 135; patriarchy and, 89; possession of, 111; race loyalty and, 9–10; racism and, 99; rape of, 89, 106, 109; sexual violence and, 89–90, 95, 100n25, 105, 106, 110, 115, 116; slavery and, 101

Black working class, 3, 68–69, 118, 121, 137, 139; improvement for, 61; intraracial abuse and, 120; narrative of, 138; stigmatization of, 120, 123

Blacker the Berry, The (Thurman), 48

blackness, 5, 15, 52, 62, 66, 105, 126, 128, 135; commodified forms of, 123; as cultural expression, 132; feelings about, 50; inferiority and, 11; non-normativity and, 120; representation of, 127, 138, 140; value of, 48
"Blueprint for Negro Art" (Wright), 71
Bluest Eye, The (Morrison), 1, 3, 5, 8, 11, 103, 107, 108, 118, 145; as communal narrative, 149; structuring of, 148; White supremacy and, 2, 6
"Books of the Living, The," 139
Breedlove, Cholly, 3, 4, 6, 40n12, 103, 149; dangerous freedom of, 108; Darlene and, 1, 2; Jimmy and, 107; racial violence and, 2; rape by, 107, 108
Breedlove, Pecola, 4, 148; Claudia and, 149; rape of, 107, 108
Brooks, Gwendolyn, 22, 79, 80, 82
Brown Girl, Brownstones (Marshall), 79
brutality, 2, 95, 101; police, 59, 105, 143–44
BSU. *See* Black Student Union
Butler, Octavia, 128, 139

Cane (Toomer), 23
capitalism, 64, 67, 79, 123
Carby, Hazel, 44, 49
castration, 89, 101, 106, 109, 113
Cayton, Horace R., 35, 57, 70, 71; Black perspectives and, 55; intraracial relations and, 56
"Characteristics of Negro Expression" (Hurston), 27
citizenship, 23, 59, 97, 105
civil rights, 78, 93n11, 96, 117, 121, 135, 139; backlash against, 140; debates about, 80; movement, 21, 23, 24, 56, 57–58, 78, 81, 82, 87, 92, 95, 97, 104, 127, 133, 134, 136, 138, 142
class, 8, 9, 13, 79, 118, 123, 138; divisions, 39, 139; race and, 121, 132

class conflict, 24; literary representations of, 145; subordination and, 121–40
Clinton, Bill: welfare reform and, 119
Cohen, Cathy: consensus issues and, 8
Collins, Patricia Hill, 99, 127
color line, 14, 53, 90, 94, 116, 128
Color Purple, The (Walker), 117, 118
colorism, 48–49, 50, 82, 145
Communist Party, 56, 70, 71, 77–78
community, 29, 51, 61, 131, 140, 147; being and, 30; Black subject and, 57; Black women and, 3; building, 41, 86, 118; facile notions of, 5; racial, 42, 47, 52, 54, 121, 127, 143; confinement, 37, 47; escape and, 33–34; intraracial debates over, 31
consciousness, 93; Black, 15, 57, 67, 80, 84; collective, 5, 149; dollar, 121–40; doubling of, 23, 79, 81–82, 121; gender, 86; intraracial, 58–78; political, 21; racial, 123; social, 20
Cooper, J. California, 144
Corregidora (Jones), 90, 91, 99, 102, 103, 114, 115; intimate antagonism in, 88, 95, 109, 110, 113
Corregidora, Ursa: Great Gram and, 88, 100, 103, 109, 114; healing process of, 99–100; Mama and, 109, 112; Martin and, 109, 110, 112; maternal ancestors of, 90–91; Mutt and, 90, 99, 100–101, 109, 112, 114, 115–16; racist violence and, 112; sexual violence and, 100
Corregidora women, 111n37; Martin and, 110, 111; narrative of, 112, 115
Crane, Helga, 43, 44, 46, 47, 49, 145
Crawford, Janie, 30, 37–38, 46, 52, 145; experiences of, 31, 33; Helga and, 49; Joe and, 34, 37, 38, 41; Logan and, 34–35; masculine authority and, 32; mobility of, 40, 47; New Negro sensibility and, 35; Phoebe

and, 36, 49; sexual awakening of, 34; Tea Cake and, 39, 41
Cullen, Countee, 48
Cullors, Patrisse, 147
Cultural Moves (Gray), 131
cultural production, 12, 28n3, 86, 132
culture, 6, 7, 15, 18, 46, 53; expressive, 14, 25, 28, 150; political, 93; popular, 122, 123, 126; racial other and, 12; White, 52

Davis, Angela, 95
degradation, 2, 13, 31, 37, 82, 87, 88, 89, 97, 103, 108, 109, 110, 112, 134; racial, 101; sexual, 96, 106
Delany, Samuel R., 128
Derrida, Jacques, 15
desire, 23, 32; Black female, 47; political, 37; sexual, 63–64, 136
discourses: antiracist, 25, 128; colorblind, 128; counterhegemonic, 123; hegemonic, 60; postmodern, 127; postracial, 127; public, 84; uplift, 63
discrimination: employment, 146; labor, 19, 59, 75; racial, 59, 60, 94, 122
"Dissed by Your Own Kind" (forum), 142–44, 145
domestic sphere, 35, 49, 84, 105, 105n31, 107
domination, 66, 140; gendered forms of, 85; racial, 114; struggle against, 141; White, 137
Drake, St. Clair, 55, 56, 57, 70, 71
Du Bois, W. E. B., 13, 15, 23, 61, 62
Dubey, Madhu, 126–27, 128

economic concerns, 25, 97, 114, 139
education, 68, 122, 124, 139; racial impediments to, 8
Elkins, Stanley, 93, 93n13
Ellis, Trey, 24, 121, 133

Ellison, Ralph, 22
emasculation, 38, 67, 98, 103, 111
epistemologies, 4, 8, 13, 122, 140, 148; antiracist, 25; Black, 144
equality, 68, 97; Black struggles for, 104; patriarchy and, 87; racial, 7, 78, 86
exploitation, 8, 32, 132; economic, 90, 106; racial, 89–90, 106; sexual, 46, 48, 102, 113

familial fragmentation, 8, 121; intimate representation of, 78–84
Fanon, Frantz, 15, 113
Farrakhan, Louis, 117, 118
for colored girls (Shange), 85
freedom, 13, 68, 92, 146, 147, 129, 130
Freedom Riders, 136

Gaines, Ernest, 96
Gaines, Kevin, 9, 39
Garvey, Marcus, 45
Garza, Alicia, 147
gaze, 3, 77, 148; male, 90; racial, 74; White, 2, 7, 16, 48, 74, 146
gender, 9, 13, 52, 56, 79, 100n25, 105, 113, 114, 118, 123, 124; Black women and, 98; divisions, 39; intraracial debate about, 85; racialized, 101
gender politics, intimate antagonism and, 48–54
Gilmore, Ruth Wilson, 44
Glissant, Edouard, 16
Go Tell It on the Mountain (Baldwin), 8, 22, 58, 74–75, 76, 79
Goode, Regina, 130
Gordon, Lee, 68–70
Gottfried, Amy S., 111n37
Gray, Herman, 131–32
Great Black Migration, 10, 21, 28, 49, 52, 54, 70

Great Gram, 90, 102, 112, 115; gendered violence and, 100; rape and, 110; sexual abuse and, 111; testimony of, 101; Ursa and, 88, 100, 103, 109, 114
Griffin, Farrah Jasmine, 22, 42

Hamer, Fannie Lou, 10
Hansberry, Lorraine, 19–20, 79
Harney, Stefano, 141
Hartman, Saidiya, 101
Hawthorne, Nathaniel, 12
Hegel, G. W. F., 65, 68
hegemony, 20, 126, 129–30
Hemingway, Ernest, 12
heteronormativity, 22, 44, 94–95
heteropatriarchy, 3, 93, 126
Hill, Lauryn, 13
Himes, Chester, 23, 58, 64, 68, 84
Hine, Darlene Clark, 80
homophobia, 8, 118, 145
humiliation, 1, 3, 4, 30, 106, 108, 109, 149, 150
Hurston, Zora Neale, 22, 30, 42, 47, 48, 144; Black middle class and, 46; Black political/literary history and, 28; fighting/warfare and, 28; intraracial conflict and, 27, 29; privacy and, 33
hypersexuality, 101, 109, 123

identity, 135; Black, 23, 48, 49; gender, 10, 23; intraracial, 19; racial, 22, 23, 50, 126, 134, 138, 144; sexual, 10, 23, 99; social, 9
If He Hollers Let Him Go (Himes), 23, 58, 60, 64, 68
incest, 6, 8, 86, 88, 105, 106; intraracial, 85, 118
inclusion, 53; Black, 18, 104; gender normativity and, 105; racial, 86
individualism, 5, 40, 43, 122

inequality: gender, 87, 113; racial, 14, 87, 92, 113, 128, 140; structural, 20, 94, 106
inferiority, 84; Black, 11, 14, 29, 43, 69, 105, 128
injustice, racial, 8, 127, 140, 147
integration, 61, 62, 63, 78, 148; Black, 79, 84; economic, 57; interracial, 64; intertextual, 126; national, 57; racial, 56, 136, 140; as self-abnegation, 60; social, 57
interpersonal relations, 19, 20, 21, 82, 84, 119, 148
intersubjectivity, 74, 91, 113, 141; Black, 16, 66–67, 70, 73, 77, 84
intimacy, 57; Black, 2, 11–21, 22, 52, 62, 74, 79; intraracial, 34, 64, 66, 84
intimate antagonism, 13, 19, 23, 90, 121, 132, 135, 139–40, 141, 148; analyses of, 20; bedroom politics and, 67; Black family and, 81; Black love and, 118; Black migration narrative and, 30–48; depictions of, 58, 87; emergence of, 22, 140; gender politics and, 48–54; intraracial consciousness and, 58–78; liberation and, 54; persistence of, 21, 112; portrayal of, 12, 78; private nature of, 20; racial collectivity and, 42; radical tradition and, 4–11; recognition and, 49, 103–16; representations of, 13, 120, 140; significance of, 10, 21, 85
intimate trauma, historical legacies and, 91–103
intraracial antagonism, 24, 25, 29, 30, 52, 58, 68, 133; Jim Crow and, 32; liberation and, 10, 54 significance of, 149
intraracial conflict, 21, 25, 30, 47, 55, 57, 86, 121, 147; art/performance of, 27; centrality of, 53 function of, 145–46; public nature of, 29; reading scenes of, 11; representations of, 120

Invisible Man (Ellison), 22, 58
Iton, Richard: on Communist Party, 77–78

JanMohammed, Abdul, 65, 66, 67
Jenkins, Candace, 19
Jim Crow, 27, 28, 29, 32, 42, 45, 53, 60, 104, 122
Jimmy, Aunt, 2, 3, 5, 107, 108, 148
Johnson, Bob, 59, 60, 68; Alice and, 58, 61, 63; Ella Mae and, 65; sexual iconography and, 64
Johnson, James Weldon: on Negro status, 45
Jones, Claireece Precious, 119, 125, 126, 133; crack addicts and, 123; impediments for, 124; intraracial abuse of, 118; literacy for, 117, 123; self-improvement and, 117
Jones, Gayl, 10, 24, 85, 88, 99
Jones, Robert, 58
Jubilee (Walker), 96, 97
justice, 68, 84, 92; aspirations for, 89; interpersonal, 20, 21; political, 23; social, 7, 44

Keizer, Arlene, 135
Kelley, Robin, 141
Killicks, Logan, 30, 36, 40; Janie and, 34–35; Old Negro spirit and, 39
Kincaid, Jamaica, 144
King, Martin Luther, Jr., 10
King, Nicole, 126
King, Rodney, 143–44, 146

labor, 3; demands of, 84; supply, 67
language, 6, 7, 11, 15, 21, 82, 91, 123, 129, 140, 145, 147; Black people and, 17, 18; developing, 126; racial, 16
Larsen, Nella, 22, 30, 43, 47, 48, 144
leadership, 47, 117, 118, 133; heteronormative, 44

Lee, Andrea, 24, 121, 133
Leighton, Tom, 63
Lerner, Gerda, 89, 106
liberation, 5, 97, 102; Black, 20, 57; intraracial antagonism and, 10, 54; vision of, 10, 98
"Like a Winding Street" (Petry), 58, 82–84
Lipsitz, George, 43, 44, 104
literacy, 92, 117, 123, 124, 126, 132, 133
literature, 52; Black interiority in, 22; contemporary, 132; as mediating mechanism, 14; New Negro, 30, 45; post–New Negro Renaissance, 57, 64; racial presumptions of, 12
Living Is Easy, The (West), 79
Locke, Alain, 45
Lonely Crusade (Himes), 23, 68
lynching, 8, 29, 60, 66, 67, 89, 104, 106, 130; activism against, 56; threats of, 58

Mama: gendered violence and, 100; Martin and, 111; recollections of, 110; Ursa and, 109
Man Who Cried I Am, The (Williams), 8
manhood, 23, 64, 65, 73, 97, 106, 117; citizenship and, 105; evaluation of, 67; rhetoric of, 105; self-conscious, 76
"Many Thousands Gone" (Baldwin), 73
marginalization, 45, 53, 60, 71, 136, 142; cultural, 120; economic, 132
Marsalis, Wynton, 131
Marshall, Paule, 79
Martin: anger/violence of, 111; Corregidora women and, 110, 111; disempowerment of, 112; Mama and, 111; Ursa and, 109, 110, 112
Martin, Travon, 147
masculinity, 70, 83, 86, 116; anti-Black, 67; hegemonic, 99

Maud Martha (Brooks), 22, 58, 80
McDowell, Deborah, 47, 86
Melamed, Jodi, 122
misogyny, 1, 6, 42, 72, 145
Mitchell, Koritha, 79
mobility, 30, 49, 51, 52, 139; Black, 32, 62; class, 39, 123, 132; economic, 36, 63, 139; intraracial, 42; masculine, 38, 40; narrative of, 38, 48
Mo'Nique, 119, 119n2, 120
Morrison, Toni, 1, 2, 10, 11, 24, 40n12, 85, 97–98, 103, 107, 107n36, 118, 144; Black suffering and, 7; masculine mobility and, 40; Nobel Prize for, 131; violence and, 3
Moten, Fred, 141
Movement for Black Lives, 25
Moynihan, Daniel Patrick, 71, 93, 93n13, 124
multiculturalism, 25, 122, 129

narratives, 9, 124, 126, 138; Black, 99, 118, 124, 135; communal, 149; isolation, 63; neo-slave, 91, 91n5, 92, 93, 94, 95–96, 97, 99
National Association for the Advancement of Colored Peoples (NAACP), 56
Native Son (Wright), 8, 58, 70, 73, 74
Negro Renaissance, 22, 28, 29, 37, 42, 45, 47, 62
Neo-Slave Narratives: Studies in the Social Logic of a Literary Form (Rushdy), 92
New Left, Black Power and, 96
New Negro, The (Locke), 45
New Negro era, 35, 46, 49, 53, 121; Black community formation during, 42; literature of, 52
New Negro Movement, 30, 44–45, 47, 52–53, 70
New Negro Renaissance, 5, 22, 28, 29, 55–56

Nixon, Richard, 87
nomenclature consultants, 128–29, 130, 131
nonnormativity, 6, 93, 98, 120
normativity, 23, 40, 43; gender, 6, 15, 21, 39, 93, 105; sexual, 6, 15, 21

Obama, Barack: food stamp cuts and, 120
"Of Our Spiritual Strivings" (Du Bois), 61
"Of the Sorrow Songs: The Cross of Redemption" (Baldwin), 17
Olamina, Lauren, 139, 140
oppression, 45; color-blind conceptions of, 24; gendered, 127; racist, 108, 146, 180; struggle against, 11
Other, 12, 17, 127

Parable of the Sower (Butler), 139, 140
Park, Robert E., 70
Pat King's Family (McFall), 117
pathology, 6, 25, 63, 124, 140; cultural, 106, 126; domestic, 122; sexual, 3, 101
patriarchy, 23, 36, 98, 106, 107, 112, 114, 116; Black, 94, 104; equality and, 87; intraracial forms of, 110; White, 64, 94, 104, 105, 109
Patterson, Orlando, 102
Personal Responsibility and Work Opportunity Reconciliation Act (PRWORA), 119
Petry, Ann, 58, 82, 84
Phillips, Sarah, 135–36, 137; flight and, 133–34
Pippin, Horace: Black suffering and, 7
Pittman, Jane, 96, 97
Playing in the Dark (Morrison), 11
politics, 15, 18, 37, 45, 96, 97, 107, 127, 146; bedroom, 67; Black, 8–9, 10, 18, 22, 25, 48, 117, 118, 121, 122, 132, 143, 145; commerce and, 36; New

Negro Movement, 47; poetics and, 25; radical, 7, 57, 141; university, 141

post-Negro Renaissance, 57, 64, 79, 80–81

postmodernism, Black, 126, 127, 128, 132

poverty, 24, 37, 40, 118, 122, 124; Black, 71, 94, 123, 132; racism and, 4, 56, 132; unrelenting, 92–93

power: cultural, 53; economic, 53, 108; political, 53, 108; racial, 14, 102; social, 108; vulnerability and, 116; White, 139

"Prayers of the Saints, The," 76

Precious (film), 118; *Push* and, 119, 120, 123, 124, 126, 132

prison industrial complex, 24, 93n11, 146

privacy, 27, 30, 33, 51

privilege, 8, 14, 61, 86, 91, 104, 105, 106, 122, 143

Push (Sapphire), 117, 118, 133; *Precious* and, 119, 120, 123, 124, 126, 132

Quicksand (Larsen), 43, 45, 46, 47

race, 9, 56, 79, 113, 114, 123, 124; class and, 121, 132; significance of, 122; space and, 30

racial justice, 7–8, 23, 92, 99; slavery and, 24; struggle for, 18, 21, 44, 89

racial oppression, 86, 99, 103, 127; legacy of, 106, 109, 113

racial uplift, 28n3, 35, 38–39, 42, 44, 61

racism, 1, 5, 18, 62, 64, 71, 86, 95, 97, 105, 136, 139, 140, 145, 146, 147; anti-Black, 30, 53, 60, 79, 94; Black women and, 99; community and, 54; divisiveness of, 116; exercises of, 143–44; gendered, 23, 94; poverty and, 56, 132; racialized, 11, 85; reach/power of, 8; realities of, 76; sexual, 13; significance of, 122; structural, 59, 107, 123; White, 35, 74

radicalism, 121; Black, 3, 8, 18, 21, 25, 133, 150; intimate antagonisms and, 4–11

Raisin in the Sun, A (Hansberry), 19–20, 58, 79

Randall, Alice, 24

rape, 1, 89, 101, 104, 106, 107, 109; incestuous, 110; institutionalized, 102; interracial, 34; intraracial, 85; legacy of, 98

Rawick, George, 95n16

"Reading Family Matters" (McDowell), 86

Reagan, Ronald, 119

Rebel Yell (Randall), 8

recognition, 21, 53, 69, 132; intragender, 86; intraracial, 113; masculine, 100; politics of, 103–16; racial, 98; resistance to, 18; White, 57, 128

Reconstruction, 96, 121

Redfield, Robert, 70

refusal: intimate, 100; intraracial, 5; politics of, 98, 103–16

relationships, 67; intimate, 84, 100; intraracial, 12, 47, 52, 56; personal, 71; semi-autonomous, 14; shattered, 150

resistance, 21, 113, 137; Black, 46, 123, 146; collective forms of, 95n16; poetics/aesthetics of, 14; White, 104

respectability, 6, 10, 19, 21, 35, 36, 43, 47, 53, 61, 98, 120, 122, 133, 138, 149

Robinson, Cedric, 4, 5, 95n16

Rushdy, Ashraf H. A., 92, 96

Sandoval, Chela: racial unity and, 9

Sapphire, 117, 128

Sarah Phillips (Lee), 133, 138–39

segregation, 9, 15, 42, 45, 48–49, 51, 53, 59, 61, 64, 65, 71, 86, 104, 122, 129; Black, 94; congregation and, 29; culture of, 46; de facto, 19, 86, 106;

de jure, 19; racial, 14, 27, 29, 45, 128, 150
sexism, 8, 13, 107
sexual abuse, 34, 88, 101, 111, 125
sexual intimacy, 63–64, 109
sexual violation, 76, 86, 89, 91, 96, 100, 100n25, 101, 103, 107, 108, 109, 110, 111, 115, 116; gendered, 115; interracial, 106; narrative of, 114
sexual violence, 34, 97, 100, 111, 117; Black women and, 89–90, 95, 100n25; historical legacy of, 110; interracial, 88; intraracial, 23, 86, 87; legacy of, 98, 111n37; racialized, 1, 98; slavery and, 98; testimonies of, 95, 114
sexuality, 9, 13, 48, 110, 113, 118, 124, 143; Black, 114, 115; Black female, 47, 79–80, 100; pathologized, 101; White conceptions of, 47
Shakespeare, William, 70
Shange, Ntozake, 85
Silver Sparrow (Jones), 8
slavery, 8, 9, 97, 102, 109, 111, 114; Black men and, 94, 101; Black women and, 101; dominant narratives of, 95; legacy of, 96; literary revisions of, 92; narratives of, 99; New World, 98; racial justice and, 24; representations of, 103; revisions of, 93, 98, 101; sexual violence and, 98; trauma of, 99
solidarity, 22, 56, 113, 145
"Sonny's Blues" (Baldwin), 8, 58
Souls of Black Folk, The (Du Bois), 61
space: cultural, 132; public, 127, 143; race and, 30
spatial ideology, racialized, 43–44
spatial relations, prioritization of, 57
Spillers, Hortense, 6, 15, 23, 100n25, 113
Starks, Joe (Jody), 30, 35, 36, 40; Black public and, 37; emasculation of, 38; gender normativity/class differentiation and, 39; Janie and, 34, 37, 38, 41; New Negro spirit and, 39
Street, The (Petry), 8
subjectivity: gendered, 99; political, 22; racial, 99; revolutionary, 67, 72, 84
subordination, 5, 19, 32, 104; class conflict and, 121–40; economic, 121–22, 140; gender, 122; racial, 19, 56, 89, 91, 100, 103, 113, 121–22; representation of, 121–40

Tate, Claudia, 15, 37
Tea Cake, 30, 39, 40, 41
Their Eyes Were Watching God (Hurston), 8, 31, 32, 35, 36, 46, 47, 49; absence of privacy in, 30
Thomas, Bigger, 73–74, 75, 77
Thomas, Mutt: Ursa and, 90, 99, 100–101, 109, 112, 114, 115–16
Thurman, Wallace, 22, 30, 48, 49
Tometi, Opal, 147
Toomer, Jean, 23
transformation, 24, 30, 42, 52, 54, 55, 84, 114, 139, 141, 148
Tricia Rose, 19–20, 84
tropes, 2, 11, 12, 20, 24, 30, 106, 126, 135
Tubman, Harriet, 117
12,000 Black Voices (Wright), 70

Uncle Tom's Children (Wright), 70
Undercommons: Fugitive Planning and Black Study, The (Harney and Moten), 141
Up from Slavery (Washington), 35

violence, 65, 66, 79, 105, 117, 146, 149; Black-on-Black, 6, 25; disenfranchisement and, 102; domestic, 8, 41, 75–76, 85; gendered, 87, 100; incestuous, 106; interpersonal, 148; interracial, 103; intrapersonal, 119; intraracial, 85, 147; misogynist, 1; racial, 2, 87, 88, 112, 115; sexual, 38, 88 vulnerability, 2, 19, 37, 75, 76, 102, 104, 115, 122; intraracial, 4; power and, 116

Walker, Alice, 10, 85, 96, 117, 144
Walker, Margaret, 24, 97
Washington, Booker T., 35
welfare, 19, 59, 119, 120, 122, 124; cuts to, 87, 146
Wells, Ida B., 56
West, Dorothy, 79
Wharton, Edith, 12
White Citizens' Council, 105
White supremacy, 2, 18, 47, 59, 82, 98, 106, 136; gendered/racial logic of, 6; textual/ideological critiques and, 7; threat to, 104; wishful-shameful fantasies of, 23
Whitehead, Colson, 24, 128, 131
whiteness, 54, 104, 107; innovation/individualism and, 43; protecting, 105–6
Wideman, John Edgar, 24, 128
Williams, Raymond, 54
Wilson, Woodrow, 27
Winfrey, Oprah, 119, 120
Wirth, Louis, 70
Wright, Richard, 58, 65, 66, 73, 77, 84; Black life and, 70, 72; Communist Party and, 70, 71

Zami (Lorde), 8

www.ingramcontent.com/pod-product-compliance
Lightning Source LLC
Chambersburg PA
CBHW030139240426
43672CB00005B/190